GONE WITH THE WINE
Living the Dream in France's Loire Valley

Second Edition

Rosanne Knorr

Illustrations by John Knorr

In memory of John, who made the story possible with
enthusiasm, creativity, and, most of all, love.

The tales you are about to read are true. That's exactly why the names of some friends and acquaintances have been changed. They'll recognize themselves but at least their adjusted names provide a modicum of privacy. One location has also been renamed-- that of a certain restaurant known for its inexpensive home-cooking, the name of which I've promised to guard with my lunch.

Otherwise this book is factual. It's all been fun (well, except perhaps for the stairs or missing parts.) And it's all been fascinating. We wouldn't have missed the experience for the world.

Merci mille fois to French friends, chefs, and vintners for everything that made this a wonderful life.

CONTENTS

PROLOGUE:
STARTING WITH GOODBYE

Everyone deserves a second chance at life, which some people call reincarnation. The trouble with reincarnation, however, is that you have to die first, then change bodies, which wrecks havoc with your wardrobe.

Our bodies, having reached the far side of 50, were not the newest models but they fit like well-worn jeans. It was only the lifestyle surrounding them that began to constrict. My husband and I enjoyed a pleasant suburban life, but it had become as repetitious as fast food restaurants. Work, meals, shopping, and twice weekly tennis matches had the redundancy of the overly familiar, a situation which weighed as heavily on our spirits as too many double-decker burgers on the stomach.

We agreed that life-stretching exercises were in order.

As further incentive, the years seemed to have fast-forwarded as we aged. Time was relentlessly pushing us in front of it. If we were ever going to begin a second life we wanted to act before our only means of travel was a rocking chair skidding across a freshly polished floor.

Thus began the dream to try a new life on for size. Moving overseas would provide a fresh view of the world, which was just what these jaded bodies needed before *rigor mortis* set in.

While we considered acting on the dream, it escalated into obsession. For five years, we read travel books, rented travel videos and pondered potential destinations over interminable cups of coffee. Country names dripped off our tongues as we sampled one intriguing idea after another: "Mexico," my husband offered, "is close to the states and cheap. We could live like royalty even if we retire early."

1

"Speaking of royalty," I commented, "France has all those lovely *chateaux* to explore – and don't forget wine and *foie gras*."

Our gourmet dog perked his ears up.

Then, we remembered a friend in Portugal – "all those fabulous beaches, sun and fresh seafood!" Another friend had raved about Italy "for the glorious hill country and Renaissance art." Then there was the Caribbean, with palm trees dancing in gentle breezes. I visualized myself, sleek as Cindy Crawford in a bikini…"

Hmmm…It was time for a reality check.

Dreaming was one thing. Doing, quite another. This adventure would come at the price of distance from our children who, although completely grown and independent, belonged to this life in the states. Our home was comfortable and we'd invested our energies in renovating it just the way we wanted it. Even that twice-weekly tennis match was pulling us back with the camaraderie of friends and enjoyable exercise.

And our accountant was a complete spoil-sport, reminding us that our fortunes weren't exactly those of Bill Gates.

Despite these worries, the refrain "is that all there is?" played in our minds. It reminded us: One lifetime isn't enough. We want another go at it.

***

The caffeine from those interminable coffee-laced discussions must have pushed us over the edge because we finally decided to put body and soul in France for a five-month test. At the very least, the switch from coffee to French wine would save our kidneys. Sure, it would give our livers a workout, but at least it was a change of organs.

We had first seen this land of wine and goat's cheese as tourists, returning four times in five years for brief vacations. One of those times, we'd even won tickets to Nice at an event sponsored by *Alliance Française d'Atlanta,* so the visits seemed pre-ordained. But the days of wine and sunflowers passed too quickly. We longed for more time to immerse ourselves in the artistic culture, to learn *le français*, and taste the joys of French farms and vineyards.

Now we began planning days spent painting those ubiquitous sunflowers, shooting photographs that National Geographic would beg to buy, writing New York Times best-sellers, speaking rapid-fire French, and, of course, drinking our share of Chinon and Champagne.

We narrowed the search to the Loire Valley, an area known for its *chateaux* but which we chose for its *agréable* country lifestyle of gentle rivers and vineyards that would supply ambiance for bike rides and painting expeditions. The area we picked was an hour-and-a-half from Paris by TGV, which is the smooth-as-silk, high-speed train, making it practical for the occasional hit of culture in the big city. And, to lessen separation anxiety, this train-sized umbilical cord also led directly to the *aéroport* Roissy/Charles de Gaulle so we'd have an easy link for visits from family and friends.

We found a renovated farmhouse to rent, which would serve as a base. We would explore the area and test this resurrected life cautiously and sanely.
We might stay overseas. We might turn and run back to the states.

Not for us, the foolhardy desire to buy a house in a foreign country just because these homes have intriguing red tile roofs, hefty wood beams, and massive stone fireplaces designed for a cozy fire. Ah, no. We were much too prudent for that.

But the house we'd rented wasn't winterized, merely designed for the owner's August vacations. It wouldn't keep us snug even in the relatively mild Loire winters…a fact we realized in the unseasonably cold spring, which one morning enabled us to photograph a May lamb under a coat of snow. And those houses we glimpsed behind the hawthorn hedges were *so* intriguing.

Long before the prudent time was up we'd begun peeking in real estate windows "just for fun."

That's what they all say.

1
SPIKES MARK THE SPOT

We begin by looking for a property *"avec charme,"* caught up in the dream of every newcomer to France who wants to transform a tumbledown farmhouse, plump with fieldstone walls, graceful arches, and a massive, walk-in fireplace with centuries of soot into a showcase comparable to *Chenonceau.*

None of the charm, however, fits either our budget or our American sensibilities. Meaning, we want indoor plumbing.

The last house we had seen fit our low budget, and the variegated *tuffeau* stone walls provided interesting architectural details. Plus, as the real estate agent pointed out, at least the electricity and water *did* go onto the property, if not into the house itself. The modern flush *toilette* sat in a corner of the garden, fastidiously shower-curtained in pink and white plastic for privacy.

Multi-list being unheard of in France, prospective buyers must sort through a host of real estate agents, individual sellers, and *notaires*, the latter being closer to lawyers than the notaries we were accustomed to in the U.S. *notaires* are highly-trained paragons of virtue who operate as official representatives of the French state and have a lock on any legal transactions with fees pre-set and guaranteed. Most of them drive a Mercedes.

Within this French home-selling haystack, we have to find the one slender needle that will have the buy of a lifetime in his stable. We make the rounds of every agent and *notaire* within a radius of forty kilometers. We can't pass a real estate office without pressing our noses against dusty windows like kids at a toy store with playhouses, as we haltingly translate descriptions in order to debate the merits of each sun-faded listing. We begin noticing others doing the same thing and develop the irrational fear that those French or Brits on holiday will find "our" buy first. The hunt escalates.

4

Soon our French is constructed from building terms. We learn "*les poutres* are strong," from a real estate agent who points toward rough-hewn beams parading across a living room ceiling. "*Le mur* is *solide*" makes sense when a *notaire's* assistant taps one delicate high heel against the foot-thick stone wall of a 19th century farmhouse. "*Le jardin est beau*" makes us question the translation when an over-eager agent describes a garden of scrawny flower beds and the dusty path that winds through them.

Our vocabulary strengthens, but our energy wilts.

Instead of seeing Loire *châteaux*, we are studying septic systems. Rather than biking vineyards as we've dreamed, we are hiking through overgrown gardens wondering if we *really* want to mow all this or should we consider raising sheep. We drop a series of agents, or vice versa, out of sheer exhaustion.

To give him credit, Monsieur Moutrier has staying power. A real estate agent recommended by other Americans, he is prematurely white-haired with the jolly unlined pink cheeks of a kewpie doll. He is a perpetual motion machine who has proclaimed himself our guide to everything mortar and stone. He will keep looking.

It has become our habit to check with him occasionally, which is how we learn another phrase: "*Quoi de neuf?*" or "Anything new?"

One day we repeat it but, unlike the smiling but negative shake of the head that told us, alas, he has not yet achieved the mission, this time Monsieur Moutrier's eyes light up like the Eiffel Tower at New Year's.

"*Oui, oui,*" he enthuses, "A special house. It's just been reduced *beaucoup*. The owners have bought another house and are eager to sell."

The reduced *beaucoup* part of the sentence translates well so we nod eagerly. Enjoyable as it can be to wander these fascinating French properties, even that becomes tiring when old-world splendor meets new world expectations and an early-out-of-work budget. Our hopes rise.

"One little problem…" he adds, as though it is a mere trifle, just a brief hiccup in the housing dreams of itinerant Americans. It seems the house is in town, with a backyard the size of a postage stamp, lacks a garage, and is four levels tall – in any language, not what we have requested at all.

John looks at me, his usual response in tight translation circumstances. Since my French is better, he is leaving it to me to backpedal out of wasting our morning on a house we have no interest in seeing. But we are trapped. We've already said we were free to see the house right now and my building-terms French still isn't up to the subtle task of backing out gracefully.

The house, as Monsieur Moutrier continues, is just a block from the real estate office, so we can walk. John and I relax. If it's that close, how long could it take?

Monsieur Moutrier leads and we dutifully follow his bouncy green-jacketed back across the town's main street, with a left up a hill, until it crosses a one-way street where an aluminum-sided building topped with a rusted corrugated roof proclaims itself a metal-working shop.

We turn left and enter a narrow canyon of two-story stone walls with window shutters closed against the mid-day sun. The only sign of life is a stolid gray-haired woman headed in the opposite direction, a faded plaid shopping cart clattering behind her. Head and shoulders bent forward, she plunges down the street, clearly determined to avoid looking us in the eye.

We pass in close order drill since the street is narrow and we all march in the middle of it. The sidewalk is meaningless. It hugs the walls so tightly that the road is the only possible route, despite the need to tuck ourselves to the side when the occasional car noses up behind us.

On either side mottled stone facades stand shoulder-to-shoulder, their boundaries lost in a monochromatic blur. I try to discern where one lodging starts and another ends by checking door numbers but fail to distinguish which window belongs to which house.

As I'm playing mind games with stone blocks, Monsieur Moutrier stops suddenly and I almost smash into green polyester. He turns and his cheeks puff out in a smile.

"Here we are."

Where? I want to ask. Before us a ponderous tumor of stone juts onto the sidewalk, obliterating what is already a narrow sidewalk to nothingness. On the right of this stone block is a solid black gate. Apparently this is the house, the one which just minutes ago Monsieur Moutrier has described as *parfait pour les americains*.

Most homes in France that are of *un certain âge*, are jury-rigged together in configurations that put a maze to shame. This house is no exception. It doesn't merely overlook the road; it almost sits in it. We want country freshness, not exhaust fumes. And judging from the one-room width in front of us, it is entirely possible that our tireless agent has finally tired of waiting for perfection and shaved a few rooms off our wish list.

John and I look at each other with a mind-reading trick that doesn't take Houdini's skills: "Make this quick and we'll console ourselves with the *lapin au moutard* on the menu at the corner *café*."

Monsieur Moutrier patters on unperturbed as he clanks through a set of hefty keys for the one that will open the gate. A blank square of forged iron, it is painted smooth, glossy black except for a few rough edges at the bottom where someone has kicked it. The only charming decoration is a series of sharply pointed spikes above the door, the better to impale anyone eager enough to attempt entering without an invitation.

It's rather Gothic in nature, this Gallic propensity for fencing homes in. Railings can be straight or curly-cued or scattered with spiked offshoots like thorn bushes gone mad, but most are topped by sharp points. I think that after having been overrun in so many wars, the French must enjoy the illusion of protection that walls provide. Like a mantra to soothe the mind – or maybe it's just to keep the local dogs off the lawn.

Monsieur Moutrier swings the black gate open.

A burly white wall on the left leads straight toward a red-tiled terrace. Everything else, overhead and to either side, is filigreed with greenery. Looping and trailing, vines spill over a slatted wooden roof and green-lacquered trellises just inside the gate. We enter through this small courtyard. Ahead, mounds of vivid red geraniums punctuate the entire length of the terrace. At the balcony we look down, down, down. More geraniums accent every window ledge below, and beyond that, a postage stamp of bright green lawn is framed by a rock garden laced with flowering bushes and colorful bedding plants. Across the rooftops below the other side of the Cher river valley is patched with squares of vineyards and sunflower fields.

We are entranced. We are hooked. We haven't even entered the house.

***

It *is* a house for Americans, meaning it has been modernized. The current *proprietaires* are a contemporary couple in their late 30's from Paris who must sell to move to a larger house nearby with fewer steps for chasing their two pre-school children. The house, as Monsieur Moutrier soon shows us, is only one room wide on the street, but it grows into an 'L' shape on the hill and occupies four levels as it drops down the hill to the garden.

We follow him through the first floor, which is brighter than it appears from the ponderous stone wall visible from the street. Facing the garden, sliding doors the full width of the room open onto a combined living and dining area. The kitchen is in the 'L' overlooking the garden, with generous windows as well. There is a storage room and a WC, or water closet. The latter is the British term, which the French, in a rare concession to their otherwise proud defense of the Gallic tongue, persist in calling the toilet. Then again, considering the historical and occasional acerbity between the two nations, perhaps it's a political statement.

A set of stairs hide behind a folding door, leading up to a small bedroom, an even smaller second room, and a full bath where one might manage to just barely towel off. Images of the large, his-and-hers bathroom with shower and garden tub that we've left behind in the states temporarily dampen my enthusiasm.

The tour reverses, back down to the living room. Monsieur Moutrier has promised that this house includes room for an office for me, an art room for John, and a guest room. We don't see where they can be unless we slide down the terrace ramp outside to the caves in the garden below.

"Ummm, isn't there more?" I mumble.

"*Bien sûr*," Monsieur Moutrier points proudly at a narrow corner between the living room and dining space. I shrug, "Well?"

He moves two feet closer to the area in question. Tucked in the corner is a skinny door, camouflaged by paint the same color as the walls. He pushes it open, revealing a tube of solid rock out of which stairs had been hewn. They spiral downwards, like the inside of an industrial-strength Nautilus shell.

Vertigo sets in halfway down, where the curve hides us from the top and the bottom, but two more steps ahead and light pours around the curve. Here is the artist's *atelier*, built under the arc of the stone cave upon which the house sits. The front of the room consists of a massive wall of windows and French doors that let in the southern light. John stands by the far window in a daze, already sizing up the exact spot to set an easel.

Monsieur Moutrier opens one of the doors and points to something outside. He is standing on a two-foot-wide ledge, squeezed into the area between the door and a metal railing on which is hung a series of rectangular plastic containers filled with geraniums. I edge onto the narrow ledge, wondering if this thing is truly designed to bear the weight of visitors, and find myself face-to-face with a Puck-ish character sculpted into the stone. Just past the stone column another face appears, this one with a serious demeanor, long nose, and even longer, curving white hair. Are they meant to personify famous personages from French art or politics? Already I'm resolving to research this bit of history further.

Through a door to the left the 'L' of the house pushes out into a long narrow room with a small fireplace at one end, large windows and a French door overlooking the garden. Now it's my turn to imagine writing the Great American Novel in a tranquil environment conducive to creativity.

Even better, the window faces my very own grape vine. Its fist-wide main vine twists past all the windows on this level and continues around the corner to wherever it is grounded. Someone, I think, should contact the Guinness Book of World Records for the record on grape vine length. I am so amazed at the sheer size of the thing that I never stop to realize that it might produce anything edible. On closer inspection, juicy clumps of plump grapes can be distinguished, a paler tone of the large green leaves. It being late September, we pick a grape to taste for ripeness and the soft skin bursts with sweet flavor. How can anything evidently this old and rangy produce something so delicious? I imagine serving guests our very own grapes. Heck, we can serve our very own wine, a bottle or two anyway.

A narrow door in the artist's *atelier* opens to reveal still more stairs. These are not nearly as interesting as the previous set, being a wooden spiral of the type popular in do-it-yourself stores the world over. They descend to a small room outside a wine cave, which in this case is truly a *cave*, complete with abrasive, damp rock walls and cobwebs. If John was happy with the *atelier*, now his eyes light up like

10

Christmas. He would be *proprietaire* of this domain, collecting wines to sniff, splash, and taste with suitable French flair.

Next to this, a long narrow room serves as a guest room, complete with its own exit via a door to the lowest level of the garden – all the better to welcome guests while keeping everyone's privacy intact. A full bathroom has been hewn out of the rock upon which the house sits. The walls curve like the cave it was, but they are now covered in baby blue tile and the space includes all the amenities. John mumbles something to the effect that "they should have left the raw stone for an architectural statement."

I envision him ripping out that fresh, easy-to-clean tile in favor of raw stone and wince. Fortunately, we move briskly on to another large cave that holds the ancient fuel furnace, a grumbling metal monster that enthralls and sidetracks him.

Monsieur Moutrier explains that the current owners, especially Madame, like their comforts, chief of which is reliable heating. Not just one, but two heating systems would keep the cold at bay. This immediately wins our hearts since the house we are renting is damp and cold everywhere except the freezer compartment of the refrigerator. Though why I'd want ice cream while shivering under five layers of clothes, I'll never know.

Huffing and puffing, the three of us climb two sets of stairs to return to the living room level. Monsieur Moutrier looks expectantly at us, grinning amiably. His hand fairly twitches to shake hands on the deal. His sixth sense has been right and he knows it.

The house is *parfaite.*

2
MYSTERIOUS NOISES AND KNOBS

There's nothing like a few centuries of history to put one's own half-century-plus into perspective. Today we're babes in arms, wrapped in foot-thick *tuffeau* stone blocks that date back 150 years.

That's according to the paperwork we receive at the official closing held in the *notaire*'s office. John and I, along with the previous owners, their *notaire*, and our *notaire*'s semi-English-speaking wife, crowded around the *notaire*'s impressive mahogany desk. As John and I put our heads together to decipher the reams of French paperwork, we came to the house's date at the same time and stopped in surprise. Of course, we'd known the house was old but we'd never actually asked and here it was in black and white. Out of the blue I recalled our previous life in which the Atlanta real estate agent described the seven-year-old home we bought there as "old." This would take some getting used to.

Later we realized that, based on the caves found in the tuffeau stone on which the house sits and the history of the Loire Valley, this property has been inhabited long before the United States was even a glimmer in Christopher Columbus' eye. Our land, if not our exact home, undoubtedly housed some of Chris' earlier countrymen. Toga-clad Italians had lived all along this section of the river. At the farthest end of our street, on the corners where the church and cemetery stand opposite each other, shards of Roman pottery and stone coffins were unearthed and now reside in our town's minuscule museum. A few kilometers in the opposite direction is a site beside the road that's bare except for two stone walls punched by black holes where windows used to be. They're stark testament to a Roman settlement at the village of Thésée and provide the excuse for a festival each September at which oxen cart rides, chariot races, and honey wine all capture more attention than the ruins.

In recent times, which in France means the last several hundred years, the *tuffeau* caves that dot the cliffs along the Loire and Cher river valleys were used as shelter for shepherds who found them to be handy abodes while keeping guard over their charges. Many of these caves have been inhabited right up to present time, except these days it's flocks of Parisians who covet them as a converted *pied-a-terre* in the country. Considering that these homes have been dug out of the very *terre* itself, this French term is more accurate than one might imagine.

Since the caves served as the original residence, and stayed in the family for generations, many of the Loire Valley's homes extrude from the cliffs themselves. The owners simply built three sides onto the front to create the "new" house, while continuing to use the cave rooms hitched onto the back. Some entrances are as elegant as the most bourgeois mansion in town, with carved wooden lintels and stone columns, while behind, the rugged cliff engulfs the house like a grade-B horror film monster gulping down an unwary victim.

Our house is built on top of the cliff, rather than beside it. Though not particularly posh, this street was the original fishermen's section of town and has been designated historic. Nothing can be changed on the exteriors except for renovation in the same style, as decreed by the mayor's office. Across from us, six houses down, one stolid stone block home still bears faded lettering in blue and salmon pink, *Huilerie.* It's easy to imagine the 19th century housewives lining up to purchase their essential supplies of oil

The street appears derelict where the stone is pock-marked with chips and soot, until we notice that shutters and doors have been replaced with polished wood or painted to a glossy finish. In some cases, the tuffeau stones have been resurfaced to pale luminous glory. Stone masons worked on one black-spotted house down the block, chipping away and polishing the facade on scaffolding that was shrouded in plastic and a cloud of dust. Three weeks later, the scaffolding came down and the results of this cosmetic surgery revealed a smooth surface of pristine white stone.

The exterior of our house has been cleaned like this and the inside has been updated. Its inner workings, however, are a mystery to Americans. So the day we take possession of the house *Madame*, the previous owner, volunteers to give us a lesson on all things mechanical. This was in addition to the two previous times that she and her husband have walked us through the house before we bought it. But between our French and the systems of pipes that go higgledy-piggledy in all directions, we gladly opt for the triplicate tour. With misplaced optimism, we are sure we'll uncover the function of all these strange gizmos.

Madame, the ex-owner, arrives amid a shaking of hands and *'bonjours'* as though we haven't just seen each other at the closing fifteen minutes ago. We exchange a few pleasantries about the horrors of moving out and moving in, translated with appropriate lifts of eyebrows and moans. Then we settle down to review the page-long list of questions we'd accumulated.

We're in the living room so we start there.

"What's that switch?" I ask, pointing at what looks like a light switch, but which merely makes a buzzing in the fuse box when pushed. Are we about to cause a melt-down?

"*Je ne sais pas,*" she responds, with a gentle shrug of her shoulders that says this is of no importance whatsoever. "It's always been there."

We're sure we misunderstood due to faulty French so we pursue the point, hinting at solutions. "Perhaps it's for a light, or a wall plug?"

Madame joins us in trying every light, every outlet, and the ceiling fan as though she, who had lived in this house seven years, has never set foot in the place but would politely join us in solving the mystery.

14

Nothing.

Madame isn't fazed. That is the way it always was, she explains. "It just makes a noise in the electrical box."

Like the old joke of "doctor, it hurts when I do this," her solution is simple: "Just don't push it."

We move on. We've already learned that the fuel furnace works off the thermostat on the lower stairwell and the electric heat pump, a modern innovation for this house, works off the thermostat in the living room. So what's this one? we ask, pointing to a third thermostat, all alone on a wall to the left.

"*Ca ne marche pas*," *Madame* replies with a shrug I'm beginning to recognize.

It's the old thermostat that worked before they modernized with the fancy new programmable one. I want to ask why no one removed the extra, but I already know the solution: "Just don't push it."

We resign ourselves to buttons and boxes with no purpose and set out to figure out the necessities. Among them is the electrical system, which we consider fairly straight-forward. We must simply transfer service from the former owner's name to ours.

For this purpose, another *Madame*, representing *Electricité de France* arrives. She shakes hands thoroughly with *Madame,* the ex-owner, and me. By this point John had left for town errands, having decided that his French wasn't up to learning anything more about the house and he just wouldn't push or dial anything for the remainder of our time in France.

Madame, l'electricienne, heads competently toward the electrical box that's inset into a wall where the narrow stone staircase twists downward from the living room. She opens the door, glances at the old equipment and sighs.

Loudly.

The sigh's meaning is clear in any language. "Tsk, tsk. This will never do." My heart sinks.

Fortunately *Madame*, the ex- owner, takes up the challenge. She and the *électricienne* squeeze into the corner of the staircase and stare at the electrical box. I couldn't possibly fit there too, but it doesn't matter since, from a dozen steps above, their rapid-fire French leaves me in the dust. I get just enough out of it to understand that the equipment is outmoded and will have to be changed.

Completement.

I wander back into the living room, pacing, wanting to know how much of our retirement savings will go toward entirely revamping the electrical system of a house we've owned for fewer than two hours. As the discussion becomes more animated, I pace from the top of the stairs where I still can't understand a word, through the living room, down the short hall to the kitchen, then back, wondering what the word is for tranquilizers in French and if they'd miss me if I toddled off to *la pharmacie* right now.

I close my eyes, take a deep breath and resign myself to being a bag lady in ten years due to the crazy whim of buying an old house in France.

Twenty interminable minutes go by, during which the conversational buzz continues to waft upwards. On each pass in pacing, I stop above the narrow stairs where the discussion has continued non-stop. I can't tell whose side is winning, but by now I'm sure that *Madame, l'électricienne,* wants to tear down the house and *Madame*, the ex-owner, is pleading for its historic value.

It's not her problem anymore but she's evidently on my side. Hoping to protect the innocent, perhaps? Or merely afraid we'll be able to cancel a two-hour-old check?

Silence.

The defending *Madame* surfaces from the stairwell and approaches to shake hands goodbye, gracious and smiling, and appearing for all the world as though she's leaving a garden party.

"But what's the problem? Is everything all right?" The fear came through loud and clear in faulty French.

"Oh, fine," she said calmly. "They'll change the electrical box completely."

I blanch. "How much will that cost?"

Like a rabbit from a hat, the other *Madame,* the *électricienne,* pops her head out of the stairwell and answers, *"C'est gratuit."*

It's free? I'm relieved but stunned. "Then what was all the discussion about?" I asked.

Both women stare at me in surprise as though the last 20 minutes hadn't happened and why would I be concerned?

Two things become clear: the love of the French for discussion and the benefits of a socialized country. We make the required appointment to have the new electrical box installed next week.

Still reeling in shock, I see *les Mesdames* to the front gate and glance at the slot that makes up our mailbox. The blocky number pasted there is '21.' Somehow this seems appropriate as a transition age into the adult persona.

No one would ever mistake us for 21, but we're muddling through into a second adult life. Our previous existence of suburban sprawl and shiny gadgets has been traded for this warren of rooms that wander up and down four narrow levels.

And we're learning everything from the ground floor up.

3
BATTLEFIELD DECORATIONS

Cozy and charming though they might be, most rooms in the house are designed for Liliputians. This makes each room seem manageable for an enthusiastic attack on mottled wallpaper and dust-bunnies.

However, knowing that large-economy-sized U.S. furniture will have to be wedged into place, we decide to strategically pick our battlefields, concentrating on those rooms that will be too small for maneuvers after furniture fills them. Those are the ones that must be cleaned and painted or papered prior to our furniture's arrival.

Unfortunately this means all of them.

With only two of us, and too many rooms fighting for attention, we narrow the field. The upstairs sitting room is front-line because it will eventually hold a burly TV cabinet and sofa that no one but Superman could move after they go into position. This room has been the former children's bedroom, so new wallpaper is urgent unless plump gray mice in pink and blue vests are the latest style in Paris.

We also plan to re-do our bedroom immediately, so we can retreat to peaceful slumber, even if the rest of the house is torn up in renovation.

Surely, we can handle two rooms in the five weeks it will take for our furniture to arrive.

Then we discover that, though bad news travels fast, our furniture won't. It will be three weeks late. After moaning that we will be camping out in a nearly empty house for a total of eight weeks, we cheer ourselves with a fatal premise: we'll use the extra time to decorate more rooms. It's much easier, we rationalize, to paint and install wallpaper without concern over spatters.

As our crated belongings slowly sailed across the Atlantic the list of chores grew. Proudly, we organized the decorative battle with all the skills of General DeGaulle planning his triumphal entry into Paris.

We didn't take into account two over-the-hill soldiers, nor did we consider the supply problem.

* * *

Decorating a house in France requires more than a can of paint and a few rolls of wallpaper. When properties are sold in France, the walls are stripped as completely as bikini tops at St. Tropez.

The general rule of thumb is, if it's not nailed down, the previous owner takes it. If it *is* nailed down, it still goes with the owner, but in this case the new *proprietaire* is left with more than a few screws loose. We are finding holes and mollies in walls where towel racks and toilet paper holders and mirrors and medicine cabinets and cupboards have been. To ensure that the walls don't look like they have chickenpox every item has to be replaced with its clone. The problem is, we don't know where those clones are being created.

Our new hobby becomes matching holes on the back of a toilet paper holder in every store we set eyes on. You'd think someone would set international standards for these things.

* * *

These details were just the *entrée* in the menu of purchases. More important were a refrigerator and lighting. With these and a sofa bed we found at a going-out-of-business *promotion* we could camp out in the house until our furniture arrived. Amazingly enough, the stove and range were built in – and stayed that way – based on our contract.

Lamps and light fixtures had all gone with the seller. The five-ish sunsets of November are fast approaching and stumbling around a house of four levels, much less working in it, isn't our idea of fun. We telephone *Monsieur, l'électricien* who, not to be confused with *Madame, l'électrienne*, is an independent contractor not in any way

19

associated with the official *Electricité de France*. He appears at our door two days later to see the work we would have for him, which at that point includes one lonely ceiling fixture needing to be hung.

Monsieur offers a business-like handshake and we are impressed with his pleasantness and practicality – he is so practical that he matter-of-factly announces that he won't install our ceiling fixture. He will come back to install the fixtures when we have all of them. That way we won't pay for repeated service calls at the house. It puts on the pressure, however, to find six lighting fixtures for four levels immediately. A few lamps wouldn't hurt either.

We put a television and VCR on our list as well. Televisions in France use, not just different current than in the states, but a totally different visual format. Two of our children had enthusiastically supported our move overseas ever since they discovered that they'd be beneficiaries of TVs and the VCR. Being the high intellectuals we are, it was essential that we replace them so as to fill cold dark nights in the country with the *X-Files* in French.

Shopping list in hand, we proceed to the first supply mission. We envision finding the ideal lamp store, which we will liberate of each and every fixture and lamp we need in one fell swoop, all priced at a discount, of course. Following the same logic, we plan to track down a major appliance store and decorating store, stocked with stylish wallpapers and matching paints.

No sweat. The shopping will be finished in one long day, then we can proceed with the work in the house.

***

Shopping requires stamina in France. Obviously, this is why most shops close for two-and-a-half hours at noon, a break that enables shoppers and clerks to re-energize themselves with a four-course *déjeuner* complete with wine, which raises the spirits more than a blue light special.

The problem with this system is that the shopping day for customers offers two windows of opportunity – roughly 15 minutes before and 15 minutes after lunch.

Our American style of shopping has so trained us in the habit of limitless spending opportunities that we can't get the hang of having two-and-a-half hours chopped out of the middle of the day. This causes us to spend considerable time trying to buy something. We understand the philosophy of 'shop 'til you drop.' We just don't understand how we can do it and still come home empty-handed.

To understand the problem, one has to understand the differences in shopping techniques between France and the United States. Besides the possibilities of 24-hour a day shopping, every town of any size in the states has within handy distance at least one, and undoubtedly many more, malls in which every conceivable item is available in any color, size, or shape desired.

In the French countryside where we live just two hours from Paris, the choice is limited by the space there is to show them, which in the villages and small towns mean one-room *boutiques* run by mom and pop. Mega-malls are as scarce as Frenchmen who don't like wine.

We need to visit the larger towns nearby to find shopping centers or commercial areas that collect most of the stores we need. Lighting fixtures. Appliances. Furniture. Various paints and wallpapers. And, of course, the still missing toilet paper holders.

But many of the stores are separated, not joined in a mall, which requires us to hop in and out of the car at every stop, in order to apply our comparison shopper skills with gusto. It's the "sure-it's-nice- but-we're-sure-there's-something, somewhere-even-better-and-for-less" syndrome.

This proves to be the fatal flaw.

Our first shopping foray enthralls us with the novelty and excitement of shopping in a different country. We wander the aisles of Auchan, a chain store comparable to a small Walmart. Here, everyday plastic items acquire mystic significance because they are labeled in French. We are intrigued by new words for picture hook and broom and light bulb.

We stop for a proper French lunch of four courses and appreciate the luxury of relaxing over our meal, after decades of rushed work-a-day sandwiches. We glance at our watches. We've eaten in what we Americans think is a slow pace but it's still only 1:30. The stores don't open again for another hour.

We sit back and enjoy the dregs of the wine bottle and order coffee. When the stores open again we're pleasurably sated with the meal and the *Touraine* red. We wander the stores enjoyably but more aimlessly than ever.

Back at the house, we're empty-handed. We haven't begun painting or papering because we have nothing to paint or paper *with*.

***

The shopping solution seems simple when a new friend mentions another shopping area south of Blois that's replete with all the various shops we'd need – paint and wallpaper store, hardware supply, a lamp shop, a major appliance chain store, and another Auchan chain store which would provide the mops and pots and miscellany required to run a household.

This fresh foray appeared promising and we set out in high spirits despite being a tad behind schedule. The night before we had closed the window shutters tight as proper French residents all do. Thus, the bedroom stayed pitch black, allowing us to sleep late. But, hey, it's only nine-thirty. We're retired and we have all day, don't we?

The drive to Blois through quaint villages and drooping sunflower fields is beautiful so we dawdle and the trip takes longer than the expected half hour.

Then, we take a wrong turn on the roundabout to Vineuil, the area just south of Blois where the shopping area is located.

Then, we drive around the shopping area itself reviewing the stores in order to debate whether to attempt hardware, lamps, or appliances first. I am out-voted on the shoe store and my husband gets extra credit for reminding me of the day's goal.

Then, we decide on the hardware store, enter and start comparing paints and mini-blinds in French.

Then, they close the door for lunch.

We skip the wine this time and nibble *quiche* very slooooowly for two-and-a-half hours while waiting for the shops to re-open…and vow in the future to always reach any store the minute it opened in the morning.

***

By the third shopping foray, we are in full swing with the system. We now know the route and return to Blois where we enter Darty, a large British appliance chain which we've seen advertised, at a respectable 10 a.m. in the morning. The store carries a large selection -- for Europe. A sea of pure white boxes greets us in the appliance section, with the only difference apparently being in the brand name applied to the front doors. Henry Ford would have seen promise here.

The prices seem reasonable based on what we've seen advertised. Even better, this *Madame*, now a navy-suited saleswoman, promises a 10% discount if we outfit our whole house in Darty appliances. We've reached nirvana and decide to handle all our appliance needs in one fell swoop. Washer, dryer, television, VCR, dishwasher, refrigerator, vacuum cleaner and …boom box.

The washer and dryer catch our eye so we start there. None of them look like what we're accustomed to in the states. We're trying to sort out the differences between a condensation dryer and the exhaust style in French and figure out which type will work in our miniscule laundry area. The saleswoman mentions sizes and spin speeds and we become involved in comparisons of price and features which, unmechanical as I am, I wouldn't even understand in English. John's

23

eyes glaze over and he wanders off to look at stereo systems. It's been an hour already.

I corral my husband in the typically polite manner of a stressed-out wife and suggest that he'd enjoy viewing refrigerators more than stereos. I gently add that we don't need a blankety-blank stereo just now but we do need something to keep white wine cool, a fact that appeals to his practical nature.

Madame follows us through the fields of white metal, patiently offering advice and considerations on energy usage and storage capacities in her slowest, simplest French – but in the metric system, which confuses the issue as we try to figure out cubic meters versus cubic feet.

I glance at my watch and so does John. It's getting towards noon, the be-wining hour, when stores close for that traditional two-and-a-half-hour lunch. Just as we're making progress, we imagine having to leave, then return at mid-afternoon to pick up this complicated ritual where we left off.

So we do what any red-blooded, American born to shop would do in the situation. We ignore the time and start serious buying.

Now it's *Madame*'s turn to look at her watch. Her compatriots begin rolling down the heavy aluminum shutters that close the front showroom windows. One by one they slip their coats on. Even our stomachs are growling, but we're in the store and have been for more than two hours of gibberish French in which we learned the merits of spin dry cycles, and Pal/Secam systems. If we leave we'll have to while away the 2-1/2 hour lunch hour then return to begin from scratch. We look pitiful.

Madame, the saleswoman, graciously agrees to delay her lunch until we complete the transaction.

"We'll take that," say I, pointing to a white rectangle that cools things.

After a three-minute review of laundry cycles, I repeat the magic words while pointing to a white square that washes things. It's quickly followed by a matching white square that dries the things the other white square has washed. Then it's followed by a black box that plays music – the one that hubby had been eying all the time I was checking out the white things.

Handshakes all around seal the deal, but quickly since, sale completed, *Madame* is ready to celebrate with lunch.

Mission accomplished.

***

Personal service comes with the territory in France, where mom 'n pop shops are still common. This requires adjustment on the part of us who grew up with stores that end in "mart" or "mall."

We still need a mattress and notice that our small town comes complete with a small bedding store that doubles as an upholstery shop. It's located on the main street, tucked neatly between the horsemeat store and the hardware store. Inside, a genteel 60-ish woman greets us politely and we tell her what we're looking for, which considering the room was packed with a dozen mattress displays, wasn't too difficult to understand even with our French. She leads us from one puffy square to another and smiles benevolently, urging us to lay down.

There's something innately embarrassing about two adults bouncing on beds and even more so when the saleswoman tells you in a sexy French accent to lay down together to see how you fit.

Therein lay the problem. I explain that our new bedroom is *petite* but we want the largest mattress set possible, even if it means squeezing around the edges of the room. The stairs, however, are narrow and we aren't sure a large mattress set would ever reach it. The king *François I* extravaganza is out of the question. We would settle for the queen-size. The concern is, would even *that* fit? Desperate at the idea of being shoehorned into a double, we insist that we don't mind if the mattress is bent gently as it goes up the stairs but, as we understand too well, the box spring won't bend.

Madame, the mattress-seller, nods her neatly coiffed hairdo gently in commiseration. *Oui*, this would be a problem. What house did we buy? I don't see that the street address had anything to do with the size of our mattress, but politely answer that we bought a house two blocks away.

"*Non*," she replies, "*Whose* house?"

Puzzled, I murmur the name of Monsieur and Madame Thibeau. Now she nods knowingly. "*Ahh, les Thibeau, trés charmants. Pas de probleme.*" She would simply call the couple, send her husband to see them, measure the offending room, stairs and window, and determine what size mattress we would be allowed to have.

We were to return in two days.

Two days later, after the usual formalities of handshakes and comments on today's drizzle, she calls her husband from the back room. He emerges, wiping his hands on an apron and holds out a hand for the introductions. Then he gets right down to business. *Oui*, he had visited the offending staircase, which he pronounces *beaucoup trop* narrow. He had then measured the upstairs window through which the mattress and box spring must pass.

He shakes his head in resignation. "*C'est dommage*," he announces, even queen-size was *impossible*. My husband and I would be a cozier couple.

If *Monsieur*, the mattress measurer, was disappointed at going to all that extra trouble in order to sell a less expensive mattress set, he doesn't show it.

A day later he delivers the double bed set via an elaborate pulley system and a ladder act that would make a circus performer proud. As he shoves and his partner pulls from inside, the box spring just manages to fit like a (tight latex) glove through the window.

26

4
RED FACES AND STAIRS

Next to our house, the one-way street is completely blocked by the welcome sight of a massive ship's container on wheels. Our belongings from the States have arrived. But not everyone has been happily awaiting this glorious day. The drivers leaving town via our narrow street are blissfully unaware. They're streaming up the gentle incline toward the truck, only to become corked up as tightly as wine in a bottle.

The two men in gray overalls who jump from the cab in front of the moving van ignore the situation.

I'm wondering if there's any regulation about blocking roads and will we be cited. It would be worth it to have our belongings, but still…

Fortunately, French drivers understand the problems inherent in these claustrophobic village streets. No horns blow. No angry shouts erupt. There really isn't any other way for the moving van to achieve its mission for the next several hours, so as soon as the back doors are opened, making it obvious that the van isn't going anywhere soon, drivers take it upon themselves to back up one at a time and sidetrack down an alley seven houses below ours.

Meanwhile I had more serious worries. The movers were unlocking the ship's container door to unveil the precariously balanced stack of boxes that hadn't seen the light of day since Atlanta.

The younger mover, lean and lanky, smiled engagingly beneath blond hair that levitated in long crew cut spikes on top. The older man, playing Mutt to his Jeff, was short and burly with rolled-up sleeves. It was he who made the business-like move and asked to see the house.

I gulped.

Little did he know he would be moving elephantine American furniture into a French house of four levels, with staircases the width of a wasp. How would I convince two French movers not to flee in panic when they saw the chore in front of them?

Twenty minutes later I'm running up and down our four levels and trying to convince myself as well. My husband, being the more intelligent of the two of us, has stationed himself at the front gate, where with a wave of his coffee cup he can direct the movers to the general vicinity for each lamp, chair, or dish box. *I*, however, am huffing and puffing while overseeing the specific placement wherever the two movers roam in the labyrinth. I'm convinced that, even if they are both male, these movers have multiplied like rabbits. When I'm at the far depths of the *sous-sous-sol*, the under, underground, with one of them and a box of workshop miscellanea, another is at the opposite end of the uppermost level complaining in guttural French that he doesn't know where to put the chair he's holding.

Half of the time the movers and I can't find each other, one having gone down the outside ramp with stacks of boxes, the other having gone up the narrow stairs with a lamp. "*Où êtes vous?*" is the most commonly asked question as each of us wonders where the others are. For the next several hours I make more trips up and down than a year's worth of tourists at the Eiffel Tower. On one pass from the ramp through the terrace I spy John, now settled comfortably into a plastic garden chair by the front gate. He reminds me that I had chosen the chore myself and that I'd also mentioned getting more exercise.

The only good news for the moving-in process is that three out of the house's four levels have direct access to the outside. The stairs that lead up to the bedroom level are the only problem, as John and I know from the mattress purchase. These stairs are totally incapable of transferring a sofa bed and TV cabinet to the tiny sitting room.

The sofa bed wasn't even a very large one, as sofa beds go. The TV cabinet was only about three feet wide, but it was six-feet tall. Not the largest in the world. But apparently the largest in France.

28

When I first expressed doubts, the movers were still fresh. The tall blond was lean muscle with a jaunty tilt to his eyebrows that seemed to give him a perpetual smile. The dark-haired man's face was rounder, ruddier, and set in business-like determination. They had barely glanced at the sofa bed and TV cabinet and it was obvious they discounted me as just another paranoid housewife who didn't want her dishes cracked. Make that a paranoid *Americaine* housewife who obviously had no experience with, and therefore no proper respect for, the superhuman powers of the mighty French mover.

Pas de problème, they announced. The items would go up the stairs, though they'd leave them till last. John and I exchanged desperate looks. Neither one of us mentioned that we'd already measured the offending pieces and knew absolutely, positively they wouldn't fit.

Meanwhile, the movers manhandled everything into the house – literally. No sissy trolleys for these macho men. This move consisted of human backs and willpower, lugging each piece to its allotted spot as I ran back and forth, up and down four floors, to have them place the items in their appropriate resting place.

Throughout the process I worried and waited for the moment of reckoning when the movers attempted the mammoths headed for the second floor. Are movers allowed to mutiny?

We were getting dangerously close to finding out. The two movers lifted a glossy chest of drawers, which was slightly smaller than the TV cabinet, but also destined for the bedroom upstairs. This would be the test case.

They each took an end and maneuvered the chest into position between the narrow walls. Two steps, then the stairway bent at ninety-degrees before it made the full upstairs climb. Two masculine chests, plus one wooden one, reached the bend at the same time and stuck. A word issued from the stairwell that I hadn't yet learned in French but I didn't store it in memory, assuming that it wouldn't be functional in polite company anyway. Grunting and twisting and sliding, centimeter by arduous centimeter, the men and their burden squeezed through the impasse only to find themselves enclosed in the tunnel of stairs with no place left to go but up.

The dark-haired one, though burly, was older and shorter with less leverage. His burnished face turned cranberry and it appeared he was about to acquire a hernia the size of *les Alpes*. The young blond looked as fresh and energetic as his hair, still a perky blond crown. He smiled. He fairly bounced. He was ready to work all night. This fact was not lost on his partner who grumbled more words I didn't know (and doubtlessly shouldn't) as they made the ascent.

The sun had gone down by now, which marked the end of a long day. Outside on the terrace, two items remained. The sofa bed and the tall TV cabinet loomed ominously like a fuzzy image of Big Foot in the hazy shadows thrown by the streetlights.

Unwilling to claim defeat, the movers grasped the TV cabinet and plunged it into the stairwell head first, as they had done with the shorter chest of drawers. It became obvious before reaching the turn that the depth combined with the height would never make the bend. The older man gave a sigh and shook his purpling face. They backed out into the living room. Our ship was under siege.

The younger mover called the older one to the cooler terrace for a conference.

"*Peut-être…*" he began and they discussed the situation in rapid-fire French punctuated by occasional hand motions which I was afraid meant blows would begin soon. They obviously disagreed as to the wisdom of continuing and the older mover was calling it a night. The younger one was still eager to solve the problem.

I appealed to their sense of fair play. They couldn't just leave us with a sofa outside and a cabinet stuck between floors. What about a window lift? Normally in Europe, movers take recalcitrant furniture through an upstairs window, just as the mattress-merchant had done. Couldn't they do that?

"*En principe,*" the elder replied, though he stated that he had none. No one at this international moving company, experienced as they were in transporting goods throughout Europe had considered that such a contraption might come in handy in a moving van.

"But I called the Paris office to request one," I insisted.

"It's not on the truck," the burly *Monsieur* growled. This was *évident,* as surely even I could see.

The crew-cut lad and he huddled in discussion again. From the body language I surmised that the former wanted to prove his ability to fulfill the mover's creed, while the latter was pleading for a chance to live.

The exuberance of youth prevailed because, he said, he had an *idée*. This was a young man after my heart – until I heard the idea.

He explained that they would simply hoist the sofa and the cabinet onto the top of the two-story moving container, back the lumbering container to our second floor window, while attempting to miss the narrow first floor roof that jutted out on that side of the house, and slide the furniture across the remaining three-foot gap between truck and building into the sitting room.

The older man's flushed face turned pale for the first time that night. So did mine, as visions of maimed movers danced in my head along with the ultimate threat of the *guillotine* should one of them die in the process. Was France as litigious as the U.S.? Could I be sued for contributing to manslaughter when one of them (the elder, no doubt) fell through a ladder rung and got hung?

On the other hand, I wanted my sofa bed and cabinet somewhere other than the terrace. I looked at John. His eyes were gleaming with boyish excitement. It was the same look I'd seen when he watched the Braves play the World Series. He wouldn't miss this high wire act for the world. And blond head was adamant. *Pas de problème.*

The truck held a rope at least. After much serious discussion accompanied by untranslatable gesturing between the movers, dark hair won the top of the truck. Blond head would be below. The rigging would run in such a way that the younger man would push each piece, sofa and TV cabinet, while the older would pull. I assumed this was a concession to the more dubious of the two, since the one on the bottom stood a much higher chance of being smushed like a bug should the system not work.

The sofa, trussed in wildly crossed ropes, began its slow assent up the side of the truck. The crew-cut blond head nodded eagerly. His plan, suitable for an elite *corps d'ingénieurs*, was working. Inch by inch, the sofa rose. Pushing, pulling. Pushing, pulling. Halt. Mid-way, blond head stopped pushing. Tall and lanky as he was, even he couldn't reach the sofa anymore, much less apply any leverage.

Dark head, lacking pride in solo accomplishment, forearms straining like Popeye's at the rope on the inert sofa, used his remaining strength to yell *vite, vite.* Quick, quick. I wondered if the sofa would become match sticks, with or without his broken bones falling on top of it.

Blond head scrambled up the ladder to the top of the container. Together they strained at the rope and the sofa rose like a beached whale being barged back to sea and safety.

The second act was the cabinet. When it reached the top of the van, the white finish gleamed in the streetlight's glow, while the two movers stood tall against the stars.

Now came the easy part. Simply back a ship's container the size of Rhode Island close enough to reach the window without going through the side of the roof. The elder balanced on the container's roof shouting instructions as the younger one edged the van rearward. From where John and I stood on the street below the gap of three feet looked like the Grand Canyon. As soon as the container was positioned, the youth sprang out of the cab, ran back in through the gate along the terrace, and up the stairs. Together the two men slid, first the cumbersome sofa, then the chest, inside. The red-faced *Monsieur* crawled in after it. John and I joined them via the stairs. The men slid the sofa bed against the wall and the TV cabinet into its spot perpendicular to it. They turned and, for the first time this night, the dark haired *Monsieur'* s face lit up in a broad grin.

Four people shook hands and the movers gratefully accepted the offer of refreshment. Even *Monsieur* of the dark hair was now our best friend. He beamed for the camera we produced to capture the proud event for posterity.

In a house surrounded by vineyards our small moving party celebrated with ice-cold beer.

5
MAKING FRIENDS WITH FOIE GRAS

We had met our first friends months earlier while still renting a renovated farmhouse. If you didn't count the roly-poly sheep John named Mr. Baaah, our only neighbors were the widow of a *gendarme* who lived in a pink house to our south and two sets of Parisians to the north, who only used their second homes during holidays. Neither was living there at the time.

Mid- morning Folly, who normally contented himself with chasing lizards from the sunny rocks and scattering ladybugs from low-lying branches, began to bark. I called to John and looked out the door. The picket gate opened. I was worried that Folly might get out, losing himself in the French countryside, so I scooped him up, and deposited him in the house. By now a young woman and man, followed by two small boys, were crunching up the loose stone path toward the Dutch door. Folly, who had stopped barking in surprise at his sudden change of location, renewed his efforts, indignant that something exciting was happening that he couldn't see. It made me appreciate the traditional farmhouse door. Split in half as it was, Folly's frantic little body quivered with eager anticipation to be out and visiting but he remained safely corralled behind the lower section of the farmhouse door, while John and I peered out the top at the approaching visitors.

The woman led the way. Her ebony hair fell in luxuriant curls past her shoulders, like the wild gypsy women the French are forever warning about. They're often seen selling baskets at the outdoor markets or going car door to car door in the grocery store lots. Some gypsy women appear outside their trailer camps, hanging the wash on trees and over fence posts, and mounds of debris seem to appear on the spot when the groups move on.

Being a strange American in a strange land, I thought about slamming the door and yelling through the closed door that we didn't want any baskets. Fortunately, even I show some common sense at times. If this woman was a gypsy, she was a gentle and well-groomed one. Just behind her, turning to encourage two small, tow-headed boys was a handsome young man about her age, with short blond hair that ruffled in the breeze. A Brad Pitt clone but taller.

The entourage saw us and stopped in front of the stoop. What I took to be their two young sons stayed behind their mother's legs, one peeking out from each side. John pushed me out the door, onto the stoop in front of him, offered up as spokeswoman whether or not I wanted the job.

Jacques introduced himself and his wife Bernadette, their sons Jules and Denis, ages two-and-a-half and five. In a combination of French and fractured *anglais*, he asked if we were, indeed, *les Americains*. They'd heard we'd moved in here.

This was our first introduction, not just to the French, but to the area's grapevine that operates on more than just wine.

Denis moved to the side and his blue eyes were bright. He was meeting a strange couple, called Americans! Jules clung to Bernadette's legs. By now we'd opened the door and Folly was allowed to enter the garden. Jules occasionally looked in Folly's direction. Folly wisely stayed out of reach.

Jacques explained slowly, with much backing and filling, since the story was a complicated one, that Bernadette's father was an American who had stayed in France after the war. Bernadette's mother is French. When the parents divorced, Bernadette was just four years old and she hadn't seen him since. In the interim, he'd moved back to the states, remarried and forgotten his French. Bernadette never knew English.

Her older sister and brother had visited their father in Florida and now it was Bernadette's turn. This little family was arranging the trip of a lifetime to see Dad, Grandpa, and Disney World. This all took so long to describe in our combined languages that by now I was beginning to wonder if maybe this family were gypsies after all and we were about to be hit up for a contribution to the vacation budget.

Then Jacques explained that the news that we were Americans had already traveled far within this small hamlet. This, of course, after just two weeks here and our not knowing a soul.

We were getting close to the heart of the matter. The cultural chasm was crossed. The topic was broached. Would I please help them with the calls they needed to make, ensuring that the family would be met at the airport by Dad at the right time and place in the states?

Ahh, now that was something I could do – speak English! Yes, I could do that. We determined that next weekend after they decided the exact plan for the trip that John and I would visit their house to call and explain the trip plans to American *père*. "You will come for *les aperitifs*, then we will place the call," said Jacques.

"That's not necessary," I said. "Really, it's no trouble for us."

They insisted. We graciously agreed, thinking all the while that it would be agreeable in any case to share cocktail hour with a French family.

The day arrived and we strolled down the narrow lane to a house that Jacques had explained fronted theirs. We were to veer to the right, past that house down a sliver of dirt driveway. When we rounded the corner we saw a larger group than we'd expected. Since the call to the United States, made officially by Americans, was an important occasion, Jacques' mother and father and one of the neighbors from the front house were beginning the celebration with wine at the plastic table in the garden.

Here began our introduction to the French concept of pleasure before business. We intended to fulfill our end of the bargain, placing the call. This was not the French system. We would first have a *kir* or two first along with assorted snacks. The *kir* is a drink combines *cassis*

36

liqueur and white wine or champagne, in which case it's called a *kir royale*.

This traditional French *apéritif* accomplished, an hour later, Jacques dialed the number in the states and I hung on the line ready to prove my skills in English. I just hoped that the wine hadn't impaired my ability to speak as a proper translator. Jacques was once more explaining what information I was to impart to Bernadette's father and the questions they had for him. I listened intently, trying hard to clear my head, not wanting to waste the family's long-distance minutes in a *kir*-induced doze.

Jacques checked the sheet of paper in his hand. He punched the buttons on the phone. I prepared to take the phone from him as soon as an American voice answered.

It was an anti-climax. *Père* wasn't there.

A friend was, however. We left a message and determined that another call would have to be made, in two weeks perhaps to ensure the final details. Would I come again for a call? asked Jacques. Of course. We arranged the day.

"You must come for *le diner*," Bernadette said. "Oh, that's not necessary," I replied politely. "It's just a phone call. I'll be glad to do it." Bernadette and Jacques insisted. If I was to provide five minutes of my time to make a phone call then John and I should be rewarded with a three-hour dinner.

***

The phone dinner began with *Montbazillac*, a sweet lush wine that slid down *la gorge* smoothly. Jacques explained that this wine went perfectly with *foie gras*. Sure enough, sitting before me was a plate on which was centered the most succulent looking slice of rich *foie gras* I'd ever seen. Heck, this was no slice, this was a slab as big as a fist. And it was mine. I tried not to drool.

Foie gras – the real thing as this was -- is heavenly. It's also filled with cholesterol ensuring that you'll get to the destination more quickly if you eat enough of it.

Fortunately for the heart, *foie gras* is a delicacy with a price tag to match so unless you're a king in France it's difficult to overindulge.

My mouth watered and I tried one bite letting the flavor melt down my throat. Then I followed it with a sip of *Montbazillac*. Jacques was right. The thick sweet wine was the perfect accompaniment. If it was a toss-up between this and sex, anyone with half a taste bud would rig it against sex.

Then guilt coursed through every pore and I paused in attacking the *foie gras*. The guilt, sad to say was not due to my knowledge of the rather squeamish means by which the French produce this delectable tidbit (the goose grower force-feeds the goose to fatten the liver.) Nor was my guilt due to the aforementioned cholesterol threatening every artery.

No, my conscience was aching because I knew that serving this mouth-watering tidbit for four was probably costing the young family their food budget for the month. All I was doing was making a phone call, for heaven's sake.

I decided it would be the best phone call I'd ever make.

Meanwhile, the *foie gras* was delightful and already on my plate. They couldn't give it back to the goose. I quieted my conscience with another mouth-watering taste.

Fortunately, Jacques made it easier a few moments later when he explained that his mother had raised the geese to make *foie gras* herself, on her small farm near Toulouse in southwest France. The young family had a never-ending supply. Guilt assuaged, I paid homage to the goose who created this delight by graciously accepting another *verre* of *Monbazillac*.

Five courses and additional wines later, we adjourned to the living room for The Phone Call. Jacques had assured me proudly in broken English that he knew enough of the language to manage the trip to the states. He just wanted to make sure, due to the complexity of telling the date and time on the phone, that everything was clear to Bernadette's *père*. We talked the plans over and dialed. Papa was there this time and proved to be amiable. I chatted a few moments, passing along the essential travel data and sending his good wishes to Bernadette and Jacques.

When I hung up, I glanced at Jacques. His face could only be described as shell-shocked. "What's the matter?" I asked. Mentally I reviewed the points I'd made on the phone, the ones that Jacques had explained. He had listened to everything I'd said in English. What had I done something wrong? Had I forgotten some essential point I should have made to *père*?

Jacques muttered something. "What's that again?" I asked.

"I didn't understand a word you said to him," he admitted sheepishly. I could see him calculating in panic. Their trip to America was just two months away.

***

What followed were language lessons via *moi* for Bernadette and a brush-up course over regular *aperitifs* for Jacques. The trip went off without a hitch. Even better, John and I later enjoyed better bread from the local *boulanger* thanks to the friendship. As they say, that's the rest of the story.

6
ATELIER DES ARTISTES

The early December sun was amazingly warm on the balcony. Not warm enough to sit outside, but definitely warm enough to put indoor projects on hold in exchange for a walk. We strolled toward town, planning to explore the streets and shops at leisure. Our narrow street led gently downhill toward the main street that curved up from the river. One block away we passed the *boulangerie*. This was one shop we knew well, having made it the daily habit to collect our daily bread. Drawn by the scents that wafted from the open window near the hot oven, we were working our way through the other specialties. We had ravenously indulged our taste for croissants, but not to be in a rut we varied the diet with various versions -- *pain au chocolat*, almond croissant, chocolate almond and apricot. It wasn't until several months later that we slowed down our binges and learned to eat pastries the way the French do, by saving this rich flaky treat for an occasional calorific binge as opposed to making it part of our minimum daily requirement.

We headed past the café beside the *boulangerie* and followed the sidewalk that ran perpendicular to the river road. The bridge leapfrogged across the Cher river in a series of mismatched arches, each just a bit different in shape and size, the result of several centuries of construction and re-construction. A small but stolid building of cut stone blocks stood guard at the far end. The medieval toll-gate watched over the narrow two-lane bridge that now carried cars and lorries instead of horses. Grey-green water frothed into brisk white caps beneath the arches, rushing downstream.

We followed the river, curved past the bridge, and wandered back into the center of town. The *Syndicat d'Initiative*, the local tourist office, occupies one of the town's 15th century buildings that are differentiated from more modern – and I use that term loosely, being centuries old – buildings by massive dark beams, ancient brick, and sides that sag like hunch-shouldered old men.

We rounded the corner to get a better look at a carving on one of the beams. That's when we caught sight of a glass storefront we hadn't noticed before. It looked like any of the dozens in town but instead of showcasing pastries or chickens or the latest postcards, these windows showed several men and women standing in front of easels. A rangy, dark-haired man, hovered over them like a *mère poule*. They were doing what people standing at easels do. In a universal sign language they were painting, drawing and generally admiring or bemoaning the work in progress.

I took two steps. John stopped. He was here in France, with the goal of learning to paint. And there, like candy before a child, was a group of painters. Ergo he wanted to be there, not on the sidewalk with me.

"It looks like a class," he noted. Sure that was obvious, but talking about it let him stand there and gape.

"Yes, it does," I agreed. "It looks rather casual. Do you want to go in and ask about lessons?"

"I don't speak French." He said, a discouraged note to his voice. "How would I learn anything?"

"It's visual. You could watch."

"Do you think we should disturb the class now by going in?"

"If we don't go now we won't know when else they'll be here. Besides, they're in full view. It's not as though they're seeking privacy."

We realized that we were as fully in view to them as they were to us. We might as well make further fools of ourselves. We entered, trying to look like we knew what we were doing, and headed for the person pacing authoritatively between the easels. .

"Bonjour. C'est un cours d'art?"

41

The teacher smiled, always a good sign, and introduced himself as Basile.

"Do you give the lessons?" We struggled to ask about the class and explain that John wanted to take lessons and would he be able to join the group?

"Yes," he said. "I am zee teecheer. I speek a leettle beet of Engleesh. My wife ees Eengleesh."

Basile admitted his English wasn't perfect, but it beat John's French by a country kilometer. He would try to explain in English and, *bien sûr*, John could join the group. There and then, John became a member of our town's official *l'Association des peintres.*

* * *

Two weeks later, we received an invitation to the *exhibition* of art for the students in John's new art class. John himself doesn't have enough art to exhibit because he's only completed one oil painting in the short time he's been in the group. However, in a show of solidarity, helped by the fact that the exhibit will be held on a Sunday and nothing else is open in the French countryside, we decide to attend.

The small flyer in my hand says the exhibit will be held in conjunction with a music recital at the *Foyer Rural* in a village just north of us.

The directions seem simple enough, though they're unlike any this former Atlantan had used before. Meaning, there's no address. No north, south, east or west. Just: 'On the main road, across from the Shell station.'

Off we go in search of the exhibition, not sure what we'll find but expecting a large art show of some sort.

We find a large metal building, modern but ungainly and ugly compared to the aged stone buildings in town. Except for the small lobby, it's basically one large auditorium-like room with high windows. On the right, a series of metal folding tables start with a

42

dark-haired man accepting money for the privilege of listening to seven- year-olds play the piano. The fee translates to $5 a person. We only came to see the art, much of which John had already seen at his classes anyway. Besides, from where we stand we can see all 15 pictures already.

But beyond the gatekeeper the tables are filled with an amazing array of homemade *gateaux*. The cakes and a wine break are included with the entertainment.

As we consider the value offered, our doctor passes through the crowd, nodding *"bonjour."* We consider the possibility that we might meet some new friends here. The members of John's art class will show up sooner or later. It's their art on the walls. Rapidly we make a decision based on negative logic. It's Sunday. Nothing's open. We're already here. So we might as well stay.

We fork over the money and decide to peruse the art at closer range. The only person we know, the doctor, has drifted off and is in conversation with another man, who smiles often. I file that fact away because it seems unusual for a Frenchman. They tend to be *serieux* and smiles don't come easily in public.

We're joined by Auguste, the large and gentle grandfather, who prefers Dali-esque designs. His latest *oeuvre* features a giant tarantula, which seems to affect its sale negatively. Auguste can speak some English, but won't. In fact, every opportunity he can get he bemoans the fact that Basile, the art teacher, tries to manage some English to John. *"Il faut apprendre le francais!"* "He must learn French" is his theory. He's right but John undoubtedly would not learn art while learning the French so a compromise is reached whereby the students speak French to John and the professor continues to provide the hints in English.

The smiling man leaves the doctor and strolls by. He notes our English accents and stops to say hello, in perfect, axiomatic English. This is Luc, the person I had called several times on behalf of our *proprietaires*. He's French, yes, but lived in the states since he was young. He explains that he's been out of town on business. He sets up museum exhibits and has been traveling.

The concert is about to begin so we take seats. The first half includes the piano, flute and guitar. Luc's daughter is the second pianist. The mayor's daughter is next. Eventually, the choral group begins – adults, all. Including the doctor and Auguste. They're good and get such applause they do it again. We feel our sense of culture deserting us as we eye the desserts and hope for intermission.

Finally, the last note reverberates and the applause is strong. We wonder how many are applauding as we are, in gratitude that we get to stand up now and try *les gateaux*.

Of all the *tartes* and other desserts, the chocolate brownies call to us. It's the first time we've seen anything like brownies in weeks and weeks. Sure, we'd enjoyed the French pastries, but these had a sense of "home" that surprises us. We didn't know how much we'd missed some sense of the usual. These are richer and creamier and so delicious we want to devour the whole platter. The rich French coffee has fewer calories and we settle for two cups.

Basile arrives just in time for intermission. Obviously, he'd been to these events before and knew exactly how to time things. He introduces another student, a fifty-ish woman with hair as dark as her husband's is white. Crystal had lively brown eyes and a round face like Mrs. Claus, but without the wintry pallor. Her face has a golden glow of someone who likes action, people, and evidently, wine. She leans over and invites us to join the group for *"un verre de vin"* at their house afterwards. All the class members and Basile will be there.

The second half of the recital continues with the group orchestras, some of whom are actually quite good. We're merely shifting in our seats from restlessness. It's three hours later and we're astounded at the patience shown by participants and audience alike. We admire the French for their culture and musical taste.

44

But we're ready for wine.

Driving to Crystal and Andre's house we pass by their neighbor's house – complete with tennis court and pool. Crystal gives us the full tour of the renovations on their *fermette*. They've renovated the small farmhouse over the last 13 years, doing the work themselves on their vacations from Paris. It's become a charming nest of floral wallpapers, beams and chintz fabrics. Crystal's hand is evident except for a marine-style staircase that leads to the minuscule second floor guest room. This is Andre's invention and he urges us to scramble up. I'm glad for my American proclivity toward wearing slacks even if most French women choose skirts.

Despite the thoughtful renovation in country antique style, the modern amenities include, not just one but two televisions. These are Parisians, after all.

We pack our group of eight into a corner of the living area for conversation. I understand most of it, mainly because we start out being the focus of attention and everyone addresses us slowly and precisely, gently cognizant of our linguistic failings. Andre fills glasses with champagne and Crystal starts passing small tidbits, refilling each tray as they're consumed. It's clear that John doesn't understand more than an occasional "*oui*" here and there. I can tell because he's trying to avoid conversation by keeping his mouth full at all times. As long the sparkling wine is flowing freely and as long as the miniature *quiches* melt down his throat, he's happy. The one glass of wine turns into several. Six o'clock turns into nine-thirty and the discussion continues. In fact, we haven't noticed any indication whatsoever that the cocktail party will break up. No one's yawning. No one's surreptitiously checking watches or poking spouses or bringing up a thank you for the nice evening.

Meanwhile, the late hour, wine, and the hefty dose of rapid conversational French is turning American brains as soft as a young *chèvre* cheese. We try our best to be polite but finally, *les Americains* become the first to rise and bid *au revoir*. No one else takes the cue. We walk to our car in a daze and realize just how exhausted we are of trying to speak French. Our language centers are so frazzled we agree to avoid any attempt at language - even English - for the next several hours. Quiet is the only cure.

We vow to improve our French or leave parties sooner.

7
HISTORY KNOCKS

John yelled "Rosanne!" in the tone I'd come to recognize as the desperate call of the male American needing emergency French translation. Just a few minutes earlier he'd disappeared around the corner of the terrace to check the mail and hopefully discover our regular copy of the *International Herald Tribune*, delivered through a slot inserted in the front gate.

When I arrive John is standing to one side of the mailbox, the gate open. Beyond it can be heard a low woman's voice but I can't see her, only John's body language, which consists of a panicked nod and tentative smile. He's apparently trying to convey friendliness in the generic sense to whoever is speaking to him, while not encouraging conversation until he knows just what that conversation consists *of*.

I edge beside him and peer out at a woman who appears to be in her early 70's, primly attired in a navy blue skirt and matching jacket. Her dark hair is a thick helmet of hair so evenly arranged in a short pageboy that it could be a copy of Little Lord Fauntleroy's.

She politely introduces herself as Madame Marteau, the previous owner of our house, a fact which confuses me at first since I know exactly from whom we'd purchased the house and it wasn't this seventy-something woman but the young Parisians. Is this some scam to gain entry and case the joint? Is this the matriarch of those infamous gypsies that I'd been warned about so often, but still hadn't encountered? I had to stop imagining devils in the closet as well as gypsies outside the front door.

As it turned out, Madame's family had owned the house prior to the young Parisians from whom we'd purchased it. In fact, Madame notes with pride of possession, her family had owned the house for sixty years. Sixty years was admittedly a mere trifle in an area where properties are passed by law from one generation to the next, sometimes for centuries, but nevertheless it seems a respectable period of ownership by our American standards. It also crosses my mind that the fortuitous appearance of Madame-who-used-to-own-the-house provides a rare opportunity to indulge our curiosity about our adopted home's origins.

I'm trying to formulate a means of enticing Madame into our lair, intending to ply her with questions, when she inquires as to the health and beauty of *"mon jardin."* I don't bother to mention that the garden she calls 'hers' is, in fact, now *ours*. I am too thrilled to have a shared interest which will provide dialog. John opens the gate wide and we invite Madame to see the house and the garden for herself. She looks shyly about, then nods *"oui,"* just for a moment."

We ply her with questions. *Madame* proceeds to unravel mystery upon mystery. When *Madame*'s husband had died she had been frightened in the house alone. This explains the triple locks, bars and various other protective devices that make our house a modern version of the fortified feudal *donjon*.

Eventually, the house became too much for her and she sold it to the people from whom we'd purchased it. The new owner had converted another house down the street into apartments, one of which was ideal as Madame's retirement abode. The deal was made and all participants were content.

Madame is a gentle woman, but obviously not shy about confronting the strange American now living in 'her' house. It feels a bit sad to realize that she still loves the house – almost as though we had taken it away from her. She's eager to talk about its history. John and I glance at each other. We'd found a gem and intend to let it illuminate our knowledge of the house.

Madame repeats her desire to see the garden. The garden? But all our questions have to do with the house itself. Nevertheless, the three of us stroll down the curving ramp leading to the yard. Worried

48

about her seventy-something bones, I remind her to watch her step, then realize that she, more than we, certainly knows the skidding potential. At the bottom, we wait for the verdict we just know is coming, the one that everyone so far has issued, the one that should have said, 'how beautiful.'

She doesn't.

Madame shakes her head sadly. Horrors, what had we done to deserve such disappointment? We are aware of our limits, with thumbs that are black and blue, not green, but when I look at the garden before me it's charming and colorful and picturesque with its solid *tuffeau* stone walls, old brick steps, and corners filled with flowering plants, all surrounding a miniscule, but lush, patch of lime-green lawn.

"*Les rosiers sont parties,*" Madame announced. The rosebushes that had at one time filled her garden are now a postage-stamp-sized lawn and rock garden. We obviously are not to blame since at this point we'd barely had time to touch the yard, but evidently she had never accepted the previous owners' improvements.

She walks onto the small concrete apron in the center of the garden and points just left of the center of the lawn. "There, that's where the pink roses were," and thus begins a litany of rose descriptions. I recognize colors and the fact that she's using French and Latin names with occasional pauses for emphasis. I get the distinct impression that she's providing a planting diagram, hoping we'll replace the garden as she prefers.

I know, however, that Folly, who had appropriated the yard as his own, would be disappointed to be stuck with something other than comfy green grass.

We're not about to tell that to Madame, however. She had literally appeared on our doorstep like a godsend and we are eager to maintain good relations. She holds the key to the house's history and its evolution from a modest *tuffeau* shelter to a four-story townhouse.

The original house had begun in the living room. Back then, the bathroom had been in the backyard, a fact we know because it's still there, the flush toilet now serving as the base for the woodpile in the back shed.

What we hadn't known was that all the rest of the house had evolved in bits and pieces. The four stories resulted by pushing up the roof, adding rooms onto the back, and digging down through the rock.

Naturally, Madame's prodigious knowledge of the house makes us remember the mysterious switch that buzzes in the living room. As Madame Gateau had said "just don't push it" but here, we think, is an opportunity to unravel the mystery. Impatiently we ask Madame Marteau, she of the sixty years in the house, she of the family who'd first renovated it, what that buzzing switch is. Expectantly, we wait for the answer.

"I don't know," she says. But since it makes that strange buzzing, "just don't push it."

***

One great mystery, however, is solved when Madame mentions that her husband had been *un amateur* of sculpture. It was he who had crafted the faces that haunted the stone columns outside John's *atelier,* the workshop where he practiced being Monet. One stone face, bore a distinct resemblance to Rabelais, laughing like the great French satirist he'd been. Another looked more like a bug-eyed Puck with goat horns.

"What about the upright large column in the cave?" we ask. When we first looked in there with an eye toward the purchase of the property, the former owner's belongings had packed every inch of what they called the vegetable cave, a few square meters next to the huge space which housed the heating equipment.

Once emptied, we'd assigned this hole in the ground to file cabinets filled with the paperwork from tax forms and businesses long gone that we hoped we'd never need again.

When we stored the first file cabinet in there, huffing and puffing at its cumbersome weight we stood up in relief. And stared in awe. Deep in the recesses of the space, where the bare bulb barely reached, stood a column. It was neatly carved and incorporated a jutting piece of the cave into its structure. Solid but decorative, the column features stone ivy twining around it about three-quarters of the way up.

We were thrilled with the discovery and speculated about the carver. Perhaps a troglodyte inhabitant from centuries ago? A Roman craftsman from the settlement that we know from the cemetery uncovered just a block down our street? Or, darn it, just Madame's artistic husband, practicing his stone carving?

If the answer is the latter we don't want to know it, but we still have to ask. We expect an immediate, "of course, he carved it." Madame's forehead wrinkles in thought as she mulls over the question. "I don't remember a stone column down there," she says. We trek down to the cave for a showing. No, she says. She doesn't remember it. She doesn't think her husband had carved the column. He could have, but she doesn't know for sure. We breathe a sigh of relief.

We prefer to think it was chiseled by a Roman, practicing before he was recruited to work at the Coliseum.

***

The Marteau family's sixty years of habitation were interrupted by the Nazis who were rude enough to requisition their house during World War II. It was then that Madame and her family hid themselves as far as they wanted to go from their home. Just across the street.

As with most places along the Loire and Cher valleys, the cliffs in this area harbor natural caves behind the houses. One of these became the family's new abode. As teenagers, Madame and her sister were curious and would sneak out at night to peak across the street at what had been their home.

51

Her face grows animated with an indignation that had survived more than 55 years. She recalls as though it was yesterday, that the Nazis had raided the family's wine cave and were passing the champagne to one another on the street.

Wagging her finger to make the point, she repeats with special vehemence that what the Germans were wantonly spilling into goblets was *le vrai champagne*. Perhaps if it had merely been the local vintage red wine, Madame wouldn't have been so teed off. But reflecting the French respect for fine liquids, she is noticeably upset that *le champagne* was being guzzled like common beer down Nazi throats.

Clearly, this was unforgivable.

***

At that time the river Cher was the flowing border between the German occupied areas of northern France and the Vichy regime's so-called free France in the south. Local resistance efforts were carried on primarily by individuals with skiffs who became a nighttime ferry service for people fleeing Nazi round-ups of Jews and resistance fighters. The groups would normally be small ones, though they would occasionally augment if it became particularly difficult to launch a boat due to a full moon or special German attentiveness.

At one time, the local priest of the church at the end of our street kept sneaking people into his church's bell tower until a hundred of them were crowded in, awaiting transfer. This made the term 'tight circumstances' literal as they squeezed next to the bells.

In reading about this tale more than half a century later my immediate concern is whether any of them ever got their hearing back.

***

After the war, feelings ran strongly in the populace against locals who were considered *les collaborateurs*. We ask friends about one small restaurant in town and the response is that "The food can be good, she's still a bit touched in the head." Then the rest of the story comes out. This was the same head that had been shaved after the war as a mark of her shame for entertaining the enemy.

Though the hair grew out and more than half a century had passed, the town passes on its collective memory.

***

Le donjon in town is not translated literally into what English speakers would call a dungeon. Rather, it's the name for a fortified castle along the river Cher built by Foulques Nerra in the 11th century. The tower and various walls remain standing though the battlements look more like blackened jack-o-lantern teeth where pieces were knocked out over the centuries of attacks concluding with World War II.

The hardy mass of stone serves as lookout over the Cher valley. From its ramparts, one can view 180 degrees along the Cher river valley, from vineyards and sunflower fields to the new supermarket, from the highway leading to Tours to the narrow dirt path that wanders along the riverbanks.

One bright summer day, we decide it's time to see the bird show held on top of *le donjon*. The advertising panels at the town's entrance advertise that the birds were *en toute liberté* up there, which we discover means that the birds of prey are let loose to fly from one leather-gloved handler to another. Vultures and falcons, eagles and owls, buzzards and even an Andean Condor, which is billed as "the largest bird of prey on earth with a wing-span exceeding three meters," join the cast.

Ornithologically speaking, seeing the various species is interesting but the real fun is due to the "bloopers." You know, like in the movies where they edit out the mistakes. Only in this case no one could edit the birds' behavior. Someone hasn't told the birds that they're supposed to stay within *le donjon* airspace.

53

At the first showing we attend a falcon decides to fly the coop and put on its gargoyle act, lording over the proceedings from a lofty stone tower across the street. The show grinds to a halt as the handlers mass themselves, shaking their leather-protected hands, flipping gory tidbits of meat in the air, making strange cooing sounds and re-positioning themselves as the falcon changes his perch. Those of us in the audience are intrigued, but as the minutes drag by those of us sitting on the stone steps or hard metal collapsible chairs are a tad eager to get out of the sun. We want them to relegate that bird to the wings so the show can continue. It's then that the loudspeaker explains the problem. If the show were to continue now with the release of any of the smaller birds, the creature looming on the tower might decide to fly back and eat the rest of the act.

Eventually, the handlers recapture the falcon, though other birds learned from the experience and periodically make their own bids for freedom. From time to time we may be driving down a narrow street and there before us is a bald eagle sitting proudly on a fence post.

Later that summer, we're lunching at our favorite outdoor café when a black shadow blows over. We are accustomed to the vagaries of Loire weather but this black cloud swoops into our midst with a whoosh and a plop. An overweight vulture, wings flapping and throat sagging, drops in for a snack on the restaurant terrace smack between the menu board and the first row of green and white striped tablecloths. Four Japanese tourists at the table to the right of us grab their cameras while the uninvited guest wobbles between the narrow aisle and the two stairs to the restaurant proper, trying to decide between the *moules/frites* and the *salade Tuffeau.*

All the birds are fitted with radio transmitters on their tail feathers so handlers can track them. A few minutes later, the handlers arrive to escort the errant guest back to his rocky home above the town.

It adds to the thrill each day to wander the town and wonder when we'll see an unidentified flying object with a man in leather gloves attempting to attract it back to harbor.

I sympathize with the birds. They're just trying to liberate themselves. Now, if they could just find that priest and make it to the bell tower.

8
MAN'S BEST FRIEND EATS OUT

French dogs attend etiquette school. As diner guests they are mannerly, polite, and congenial. This fact becomes evident the first time we dine at the local *crêperie*. A massive lump of black and brown fur that is decidedly more German shepherd than French poodle takes up most of the space beneath his master's table, next to his master's hiking boots.

We shrug. This is acceptable in France, though not normal for Americans. It's fascinating to watch the dog, head on paws, eyes clear and watchful, and not a peep out of him. In this gourmet capital of the world, dogs dine well and when they join their people in *les cafés* the proper French dog knows enough to make himself unobtrusive for the duration. It has to be an exercise in will power because we humans can hardly withstand the delicious aromas wafting from the kitchen. I don't know how our four-footed friends manage.

Though we discovered dogs under the tablecloths in most French restaurants, even some of the better establishments, we aren't about to enter one with Folly in tow. The *crêperie*, however, has proven itself hospitable so one evening we invite our loyal pup to join us. His eyes glitter when he sees the leash. He's coming with us to dinner. Yes! He fairly prances down the street and we lift our heads high, sure that we look especially French, though I doubt that the French feel as we do when we arrive at the restaurant's front door. Our American brains rebel at the thought of taking a dog inside. It becomes an effort of will to cross the threshold, sure that some manager will pounce on us with derision, citing twenty city, county, and state regulations against the germs on four paws.

Nothing happens. We scan the room. Only one table is occupied at this early hour and the young couple barely glanced up.

The waitress enters from the double doors to the kitchen and merely nods, acknowledging our presence with a quick "*Bonsoir.*"

We quickly install ourselves at a corner table, where we can be unobtrusive until we – and Folly – get the hang of this. Already he's bouncing like a ping-pong ball at the excitement.

The novelty causes his humans to be ceaselessly aware of Folly's presence under the table -- that and the fact that, instead of lying down quietly like French dogs, our American version is standing at full alert. We tell him to lie down and he won't. We push down on his tiny behind to make the point and he sits. The minute we turn our attention back to the menu he stands up again. We repeat the process.

Finally we give up. We tell ourselves that if a dog wants to exhaust himself by standing for an hour-and-a-half that is his problem. We, however, do not forget his presence and lavish small attentions on him, sharing a special table treat now and then.

To say Folly enjoys this attention is understatement. He is fully engaged in the new routine and accepts it with enthusiasm. Very quickly he assumes that. if food is not continuously forthcoming, he's been forgotten. This requires a reminder. Just a gentle nudge with a paw on the knee. Still nothing? A few more nudges. If the people above that tablecloth are too busy talking to notice him, then a polite yip is designed to attract their attention to the starving puppy who had eaten a mere two meals and four snacks so far that day.

It's an understatement to say that when we compare the mannerly French pooches with their distant American cousin, Folly, he fails.

But it gets worse. Folly has figured out that the food is with us and he is with us so the food should be with him too. The whining starts very low. Only John and I can hear it. In the interest of keeping the peace, we provide a piece of *crêpe* to fill his mouth. When Folly's yips become barks and his paws begin wearing a hole through my jeans, we realize we'd created the doggy equivalent of an ugly American.

***

Fortunately, Folly has redeeming features. In a country that loves dogs of all persuasions, his soft white fur and big brown eyes stop old women and small children in their tracks. He quickly learns that "*Comme, il est mignon!*" means he gets petted behind the ears.

Other than the failed dinner out, Folly adapts to France wholeheartedly. This is not surprising, since what dog would complain about living in a country filled with *paté* and *foie gras*. This had been the original bribe. When we flew over to France we had told him in all earnestness that if he would just behave on the plane he would get *paté* as his award. When he curled up in his carryall in the cabin and slept quietly for the eight hours, we had new evidence of his intelligence.

Folly is often treated as an honored guest. After the failed restaurant experience, we still brave a sidewalk café now and then, since being outside with coffee gives Folly less to whine about. The waitress brings our order and returns with a refreshing bowl of water for Folly. The top place in our doggy star rating system goes to an unpretentious café on the French *autoroute* leading to Provence. John and I, as mere humans, followed the regular routine of going through the cafeteria line to order coffee and croissants. I spy a corner table and leave John to pay and gather our things while I keep Folly out of the way and *tranquil.* I sit down and soon see John trotting back with our breakfast tray.

He no sooner sets it on the wooden table than we notice the counter waitress following in his wake. John and I look at each other. American habits of decades forget for the moment that we are in France. Our panicked thoughts take on staccato form. In order, they are: Dog. Restaurant. Thrown Out.

But the young *serveuse* is carrying a tray and smiling. As she draws nearer we blink and look again at the tray's centerpiece. With

58

personal attention worthy of the finest dining establishments, she is serving Folly a bright red bowl of a dog's best vintage -- water. It is accompanied by two doggie biscuits, neatly presented on a white paper napkin.

Michelin, eat your heart out.

9
KISSING LESSONS

Marie-France said, "Kiss me again."

We were about to leave a soiree given by new French friends. I stopped in mid-goodbye and stared in mute shock. Had I misunderstood the French words? Thoughts of alternative lifestyles flick through my head. I don't know these people very well. Are they all, well, libertine? Hmmm. Difficult to imagine that of Marie-France. Just how kinky could this lively, but matronly figure of a French woman – right down to the prim French twist of her white hair -- *be* anyway?

While I ponder, the room quiets. It's not exactly reassuring to realize that everyone else is as puzzled as I am. The guests stop in their own mid-puckers and create a frozen *tableau* around us, all eyes focused on Marie-France and I in the center.

It was the end of a pleasant evening. Our intimate group numbered seven: Marie-France and Michel, our hostess, Annick, two other widows, Odile, and a Dutch woman, Pieta, John and I. The group has been convivial and smiled as heartily as they dined. John and I smiled back between delicious bites but unfortunately we lost about 90% of the conversation that bounced across the table as rapidly as a tennis ball at the French Open. These people are good friends and, even if we'd known the language better, I was sure we wouldn't have understood some of the allusions to neighbors or town politics. Nevertheless it was a small step in our acceptance and we felt fortunate to have been invited to join them. But by ten thirty we are replete with food and wine, exhausted by the strenuous efforts as socializing in a foreign language, and ready to go home.

It took an hour longer for our new French friends to come to the same conclusion.

It's with relief that we note people begin to pass coats to their owners. Goodbyes begin slowly, then gather steam until the seven guests are totally engrossed in the ritual of shaking hands or providing *les bisous* to each and every combination of people. *Bisous* are the cheek-brushing kisses passed around promiscuously during French greetings and goodbyes. I wonder how they can remember, by the time they make the rounds of seven people after a thoroughly wine-imbued dinner, who they've already kissed and who they haven't and if this could be a case of the endless kiss. Instead of the man who never returned from the MTA, in this case we might never return from the French *soiree*.

Marie-France repeats her request in a determined voice and adds something that I take to mean my cheek kissing technique is not up to snuff. I look at John who has already provided his version. Marie-France didn't say a word to *him*. Although she delicately avoids saying so, it's evident that my puckers put me somewhere in the category of a guppy.

I peck sheepishly at her check for a second goodbye *bisous*. "*Non. Encore*," she says. My MTA analogy begins to appear closer to reality.

My new friend, this cheerful *femme française*, could no longer stand by helplessly while the resident *americaine* botches the French *bisous*. She explains that I need training.

Marie-France begins the instruction. "Do not pucker. Just poof…" The group surrounding us adds coaching from the sidelines.

Even my American husband joins in. He's smug. After all, he might not speak French very well, but something as vital as kisses…well, of course *he* knows the proper technique. Doesn't everyone? I glare at him.

Marie-France stands waiting. I repeat the action requested, a dozen times. Poof, poof. Again. Poof, poof. Just miss the cheek. Poof poof.

I still don't know if I learned the proper technique or if Marie-France simply gave up in the interest of allowing everyone who was gaping at us to leave at a decent hour.

***

If the French art of *bisous* were a sport, the training would be of Olympic proportions. The practical application requires learning which players should be included in the match, when to pursue the partner, whether to start with a right or left cheek scrimmage, and how to determine the number of kisses required to reach the goal.

Eventually my technique improved but I'll always be puzzled as to the correct number of alternating pecks on the cheek to apply. The number can vary from two to three or even four. Even a novice realizes that one peck is miserly. If you know someone well enough to pucker, then go for one more. Therefore, two pecks are common. Three are for close friends. Four are applied by the extravagant and often catches even the practiced French person off-guard. It was a great consolation the day a French woman admitted that even she could be puzzled when dealing with a new friend "especially if they're Parisian," she said. That explained everything.
***

Of equal importance to the *bisous* in France is the ritual handshake. The actual technique is not a problem, since handshakes are the same in France as in the United States. It's knowing *when* to clasp hands that requires training.

In France it boils down to this: Any time that you're not kissing, you're shaking.

John and I were particularly impressed by the French culture, which emphasizes both *la politesse* and *la fraternité*. A French person considers himself rude if he does not acknowledge a friend, acquaintance or the local café owner whenever they're encountered. A handshake and a few words are the minimum. Of course, based on the

French love of discussion the brief exchange leads to more words on the changes in the mayor's office or the quality of the new butcher's offerings. Forty-five minutes later, the hello is ended with a goodbye clasping of hands.

This is why one is never bored in France. Between the kisses and the hand shaking, just running down the street for bread can take all morning. When pressed for time, I've considered wearing dark glasses and a wig.

In a group situation, handshakes are *de rigueur*. John learned this much later when he learned to play the bocce-like game of *pétanque.* The game is held informally at a local park and players try to arrive at the stroke of two. But it's not unusual for arrivals to be staggered over the next hour. Often the teams are arranged, the wooden target is in place, the metal balls are lined up, and one of the players is in position to throw the ball when one of the usual players walks in late.

Play halts as though a curtain had been drawn over the playing field while the newcomer makes his rounds to each of the three teams, shaking hands with each of the four or six people on the team. *Les boules* lay forgotten in the dust.

One day we were sitting in the local bar when the owner recognized someone sitting at a corner table near us. He nodded to him and went over to shake hands. He couldn't leave it with that, however, because even if he knew no one else personally at the table or in the room, he felt obliged to include them. Thus begins the round of handshakes for everyone at that table. But, one person is sitting nearby at another table, so he includes him. Of course, our table is near that man's, so the owner includes our group as well. Eight people, that day, if I recall. The next time we show up at that bar, it means we had all reached shaking status. From that point on the owner would rush over, hands outstretched and we begin the rounds again.

***

With all this kissing and handholding we often wondered how the French handle the issue of sexual harassment. This was a current issue when we left the United States, with Hollywood covering the subject in several movies. That made it very hot stuff.

In France it doesn't translate.

When Annick (the hostess of the infamous kissing lesson *soirée* above) and I were lunching later she didn't see what the fuss was about. "A woman must be appreciated," she says. "How else can a man show it?"

An American friend, a businessman transferred to France, admitted that he was at a loss as to how to proceed. "I took all that U.S training they give you on how not to harass, even innocently," he said. He had learned to avoid personal comments and stick strictly to business. But as polite as he was to his secretary she looked more and more bereft as the weeks passed.

Was it something he'd said in his newly acquired French? The opposite. He'd been too reticent. "I discovered that my secretary was insulted if I didn't comment on her new dress or hairdo."

He could speak French. He just couldn't figure out what to say to women.

10
EVERYTHING IN ITS SEASON

Friends from the states will be taking advantage of our guest room, starting next week. They'd never been to France and we're eager to introduce them to everything we love about the country. I begin reviewing recipes, planning menus for our meals *en plein air*. But it's the settings that impress me the most. I'm particularly awed by one cookbook with photos of rustic picnic settings, softly sun-glazed and hazy as though basking in summer heat. The food is almost incidental to the décor, which sings of French country life. The wooden tables are set with luminous red, blue and yellow patterned cloths.

Vital to the scene are bright pots of geraniums. They appear in profusion, scattered artfully about the scene, pretending that no guile is involved. Sure, some art director took six hours to place each pot, turn each arrangement to its ideal angle, but those bright pots of geraniums become essential to my image of the proper *terrasse* ambiance. With my cooking skills, subterfuge is even more essential.

I must create a setting that will impress American guests with the charms of a French garden lunch.

Never mind that it's early March in the Loire and not July in Provence. Despite the fact that I'm still wearing my insulated coat, I'm optimistic that the southern sun will pound straight down on our whitewashed terrace. It's protected from the wind on three sides so with the sun, it's always ten degrees warmer than anywhere else in the yard. From the terrace railing, one can look down to the flowering bushes in the rock garden and the postage stamp of green grass that is *le jardin.* It's pretty enough. All I need do is buy those lovely bright red geraniums for the window boxes that line the railing. They were lush beacons when we first bought the house last October. They overflowed their rectangular bins and brightened up the solid stone walls. Even I, lacking a true *main verte* that I am, can succeed at it. Or so I thought.

At the weekly market in town one young woman is selling the colorful early spring *primeveres,* that thrive on cool nights and shady days. Very pretty, but small, and not the bright ruby geraniums I am craving. When I explain what I want, she points across the river where the tops of greenhouses peek above the trees. *Oui*, they would have geraniums later. I didn't catch the subtlety in her response that they "would" have "later."

I drive down a rutted dirt road. Just before it peters out in a field, I reach an even more rutted dirt driveway. At the end of it are six greenhouses, three on each side. No one is in view but the sign indicates that this is the place and the gate is open.

I get out to look around. Ahh, there are my geraniums. Three of the greenhouses are packed with them. Thousands of the darlings are lined up in neat green lines speckled with dots of red. Those dots will bloom soon, just in the nick of time, in fact. I can already hear my friends enthusing over the glorious spill of color in my backyard. I can see myself at home this afternoon, gently planting each one with my newfound talent for nurturing young plants.

A dark-haired young man walks toward me. I guess he might be the young woman's husband -- certainly he belongs to the place. The rich humus on his plaid-shirt and under his fingernails is a distinct clue. *Je peux vous aider?* he asks.

"*Oui*," I tell him, "I'd like some of those. The geraniums." I point through the door of the closest greenhouse and walk toward them, eager to begin the selection process. Hmmm, how many will I need for six window boxes?

"*Non*," he says.

"No?" Not even I could have misunderstood the simple word. My French isn't *that* bad. I know my green thumb is black and blue, but is that any reason to refuse to sell me his precious plants? I stand my ground and ask again.

"*Non*," he explains, "You cannot buy them now. It is too soon."

"It's *not* too soon. I have guests coming next week."

"You can have the large geraniums in two weeks. The small ones, those you have in four weeks. Come back then."

Rows of geraniums create lines of bright red under three white plastic-ceiling tents. They are sitting there, just waiting to be sold and this man is pleasantly telling me I can't buy them. I've never been to a store where anyone refused to take money for merchandise. In the large chain garden store around the corner from my home in the states I've never had anyone tell me I couldn't buy *anything*. It's positively un-American. Even if the merchant thinks the plants would die an early death, that's good for the store. They'd just sell me more to replace them. It's free enterprise.

"I'll take the chance now," I offer.

"*Non*, it is too early." He smiles and seems pleasant enough but the gardener holds his ground. "Come back in two weeks," he repeats. The large ones could be planted then. If I wanted to save money, I could wait four weeks and he'd sell me the small ones that were less expensive. They'll grow. But he's not about to sell me premature geraniums that can't survive into summer. He'd rather lose the sale today than lose his reputation by selling plants before their time. Besides, I, his client, would waste her money.

Integrity like that must be rewarded. As I drive off that's exactly why I *would* return.

***

Three days later the sun comes out. The terrace is warm enough to sit outside. In a sweater. For ten minutes.

But there are no geraniums. Without them the boxes hanging from the balcony are naked except for the dredges of old roots and dirt from past glories. Below, the garden is bald except for the green hedge and ivy trailing across the stone walls. It's against my new homeowner's nature to let guests see this empty landscape when I knew how beautiful it could be.

Back I go to the garden shop across the river. The *pensées* are here and I know those are available. The young woman was selling them in the market. The small bright plants look like pansies, but what would I know?

I look longingly in the direction of the geraniums. I even offer another plaintive request to buy some. I already know the answer. "*Pas maintenant.*" I can't buy them yet. So I proceed in stuttering French to request the other plants, *les pensées*. The young man in his plaid shirt is as patient as a pediatrician providing a new mother with care instructions for her babe. He kneels beside the bedding plants and explains slowly. I should place them in the sun now, he says, and water the little ones well. But to ensure their health and long life I should replant them in a few weeks when the sun gets too warm. Move them to a shadier spot.

Then I can buy the geraniums to take their place. He's gone from pediatrician to parent mode now, filled with pride at the offspring he's produced. Finally, as a special treat, he lets me enter the nursery with the geraniums. The greenhouse smells of the sweet, damp humus. The baby geraniums and their parent plants display the family tree of the geranium world. Under the translucent white tent are red, rose, white and multi-hued geraniums. Some have broad flowers, others are made up of several small blooms. The gardener leads me from one to the other, explaining the marvels of each type. This one is good for an upright container. That one will gracefully fill in a window box, bending slightly to show the blooms from below so it's the best choice for balconies. That one is a new variety with a pointed leaf, but *bien*

68

sûr, it's a geranium. He moves from a beauty in a vivid rosy-purple shade to a red blossom with petals like velvet, then a white flower with a dramatic crimson center. All are lovely. The choice is magnificent.

But, *non*, I still can't buy them now.

***

The greenhouse lessons in geraniums and *pensées* have increased my gardening knowledge by a sprig. That's not much because in France one doesn't settle for a green thumb, one's whole hand becomes *une main verte*… or nothing. Having spent my adult life entirely within the confines of an office except for a few brief episodes of mowing grass, I'm more successful at over-watering, under-watering, confusing sun-loving plants with shade-lovers and, in general, creating brown stumps where green should be.

Despite my lack of ability, the geraniums thrive thanks to the bright Loire sun and, undoubtedly, to the fact that the purchase had been forbidden until it was bright enough.

Le jardin is full of surprises. As the first weeks of summer arrive, bushes that were brown sticks leaning against a curve of stone wall show a hint of yellow. I don't investigate because the incessant spring rain (yes, the same rain that makes this the Garden of France) keeps us indoors. Days later I wander to the edge of the terrace and the garden is transformed. The shy yellow buds have flowered into a profusion of dainty blooms that look like miniature chrysanthemums. Bright red tulips are waving gaily on their stalks in an otherwise barren corner I'd never noticed before. The crevices in the rocks leading down the steps are filled with bits of foliage that's speckled with dainty purple flowers. I don't know the names in English, much less in French, but it doesn't take language skills to enjoy them.

We're such innocents when it comes to what everyone else seems to take as the seasons of life. Later in the summer we take bike rides and discover patches of blackberry bushes. We begin to carry small plastic containers to collect them. Once we know what to look for, they appear everywhere but they're profuse along the dirt path beside the river. We carry *bigger* plastic containers. That's when we get fussy and begin comparing for quality and quantity of fruit.

We notice strange balls of vegetation, a foot-wide in diameter, stuck up in the still-bare plane trees throughout the Loire Valley. A stork nest? But that's a lot of storks and we haven't seen a one of them.

Finally, the mystery is solved. It's mistletoe. Never have we seen it outside of December and we thought it grew in small sprigs with red ribbons attached by which it's hung over heads.

If it's true that one should kiss under mistletoe we now know why the French do all those *bisous*. They stand under that stuff every day.

***

When I'm in the garden, I have a better view of the bourgeois house next door. Outrageously tall, it towers over our house like a parent beside a toddler. The house is elegant in blocks of clean creamy stone with cinnamon colored shutters pierced by a filigree design.

The back of the house is best of all. Over the lintels on two floors are carved designs. One features a gnome-like figure, another is an ornate column, and on yet another column leading down to their garden sits a three-foot high *grenouille*, a gigantic frog with a smile as though he'd just eaten the world's biggest fly. Pitted by time, he reigns like a glorious prince on his stone pedestal without a pond.

The house is a *grande dame* itself but it's also inhabited by two *grandes dames* of a certain age. When we first moved into our house, the former owners explained that our neighbors consisted of a mother and daughter who lived in the family home.

A woman with beautifully coifed silver hair, who appeared to be in her late sixties, would enter or leave that house but we never had opportunity to meet her. We never did see her daughter and were curious about the family who had become our neighbors.

One day, I'm coming out my door just as *Madame*, our neighbor, is leaving to walk to town. We nod hello and introduce ourselves. As we part she suggests that we should meet her *Maman* someday.

Oops. I'd met the *daughter*.

A few days later, I'm working in the garden when John calls that the electricity is out. He can't blame me; I wasn't digging with anything at the time, just weeding. We hold a brief confab, wondering if the electrical problem is only ours, or a general problem. We hope for the latter, of course. To enlighten ourselves, I volunteer to ask *Madame* next door.

I knock on our neighbor's front door, secretly glad for the excuse to sneak a peek inside the house. Despite my unexpected arrival, *Madame,* the daughter, appears as though she's expecting company. Her glossy blonde (dyed to tastefully cover the gray) hair is perfectly coifed. Her green print dress is conservative but tastefully styled with neat white piping around the sleeves and down the bodice. Her mode of dress and level of perfect grooming are the sort of thing I'd reserve for dinner out – well, on my birthday. A decade birthday. Maybe, if it was a good hair day.

The wide front hall is floored in black and white parquet patterned tiles. The ceiling is high, at least ten feet, probably more, and lining the walls are oil paintings in ornate wooden frames. A glass-front étagère showcases small collectibles in silver, china, and crystal. Even loving the frog that ate Cleveland from the outside has not prepared me for the inside. I am thrilled. I want to wander through the house and study every corner. I shouldn't stare though. Would she please leave so I can wander to my heart's content?

We chat briefly. The electricity is out, *oui*, even here. Then the miracle occurs. "Would you like to make the acquaintance of

Maman?" she asks. I would. indeed. I want to venture past the entry hall and delve further into the realm of antiquities and cultured French home life. Then I look down at my sweatshirt and jeans with the sudden desire to ask if I could go home and change first.

Maman, in her late 80's, is a tiny bird of a woman, elegantly coifed for a woman who is supposedly ill. Either these two women had a personal hairdresser hidden in the house or secrets I would never know for controlling hair. Every silvery hair gleams above her royal blue dress. Now I feel like the garbage in the midst of royalty. I vow to clean up my act. But if *Maman* notices, she doesn't mention my workday attire as we chat. She's lively and personable. I never do discover her name, since she is introduced as *Maman* and *Maman,* she says, is what I am to call her.

Since meeting her in person, *Maman* seems to take a friendly interest in us. Now and then she ventures out onto her terrace and waves from on high, regal as British royalty. I wave back. Meanwhile, *Madame*, her daughter, works in their garden under *Maman*'s encouraging eye. Rake in hand she combs the chocolate brown earth. From my eagle's perch on the terrace every neat row the tines make stand out in high relief, perfectly aligned. They're as neat as Madame herself. For gardening she's wearing a beige cardigan sweater set, black and beige plaid skirt – and black pumps with stacked heels. Watching her is the equivalent of seeing a television commercial from the sixties that shows a housewife cleaning her kitchen floors in two-inch high heels.

I look down at my rumpled sweats, wishing she couldn't see me working in the garden nearly as well as I can see her.

11
THE PERFECT BAGUETTE

Six days a week I'd push open the door to the *boulangerie* and say the requisite *'bonjour,'* receiving the habitual *'bonjour'* in reply. But the rotund young woman behind the pristine white counter wore her apron like full-body armor and never cracked a smile.

We continued this routine day after day. Meanwhile, the friendship with Bernadette and Jacques grew. To further their plans to visit dad in Florida, we continued an exchange that combined social occasions with English lessons, French lessons, and wine.

One Tuesday, which just happened to be the day of rest for our *boulangerie*, Bernadette and Jacques biked by the house. Denis was on his small bike in front of them. Jules was seated behind Jacques. Would we like to join them for the ride to the lake nearby? Gladly.

It was one of those days when the sky is blue, clouds are few and fluffy, birds sing…and the resident baker's clerk takes a day off. *Madame* from the *boulangerie* was fishing with her husband and looked up as we rolled to a stop. Bernadette waved and Madame strode straight toward Bernadette and Jacques. We saw more of her teeth than we'd ever seen before as she beamed. The three adults greeted each other with *bisous* all around. Then the bakery *Madame* bent to offer *bisous* to Denis and Jules. We watched from the sidelines. When the official greetings were complete Bernadette took me by the arm and began the introduction. Surprise crossed the bakery *Madame*'s face, as though John and I had suddenly materialized from thin air.

She muttered something that sounded like *ah, oui, les Americains* and shook hands politely. After a bit of chat, mostly between Bernadette and the bakery *Madame*, we separated, *Madame* back to her fishing pole and our small group to complete the circuit of the lake. We returned home without seeing Madame again that day.

But that brief encounter was to have important repercussions at the bakery counter.

The next day when John and I entered the *boulangerie* Madame nodded her usual *bonjour* then added a comment on the cloudy weather. Apparently we were not non-entities any more. We'd been appropriately introduced. Little did I know that the goal of total acceptance was still to be achieved.

During the next several weeks, the bakery *Madame* and I exchanged pleasantries as best we could, based on my awkward French and her influx of customers, who occasionally lined up as far as the front steps. Then came the big event for Bernadette and Jacques – the family trip to Florida, the tale of which made the rounds in town. Everyone knows that *les Americains* had made the phone calls, helped Bernadette and Jacques with their English, and apparently had become very close with the family, who were valid French members of the community.

Then one morning bright and early John drops me off at the bakery to pick up a fresh baguette for breakfast. I open the door and Nathalie, Bernadette's teenage daughter is just turning away from the counter with their family's bread.

"Nathalie, *bonjour*! How was the trip?"

She beams. "*Magnifique!*"

We share *bisous* and, since the bakery is otherwise empty, we stand by the front door chatting about the trip to see *grandpère*, the day at Disney World, the visit to the Everglades. I am facing the counter and, behind Nathalie's enthusiastic nods and a discussion of the teen joys of shopping for Levis, the bakery *Madame* is watching with interest.

In a fifth dimension I sense the wheels turning in her head, following a logical path. I know the family well. I'm on *bisous* terms. I had been coming into this bakery for months now. Apparently I am not going to disappear from the village anytime soon. I am, ergo, a regular customer.

After the goodbye pecks from Nathalie, I return to the counter and order our usual *baguette*. Madame nods, *oui*, and turns as usual toward the sticks of fresh bread stacked on the shelves behind her. But she doesn't simply grab a *baguette* from the front of the stack as I expect. They look fine and fresh though one had a small bump on its left side that marred the symmetry. Nor does she choose any of the other baguettes in full view along the front row. Delicious, I am sure, but a little light or a little dark.

Instead, Madame performs an act of prestidigitation worthy of Houdini. Her nimble fingers sneak carefully around the back of the stack. They bypass the sticks of bread that look delicious, despite modest imperfections, and present me with one evenly browned, symmetrically oval, picture-perfect French *baguette*.

I could hardly wait to pay my francs and rush to the car to let John know: "We've arrived."

12
PLAYING THE MARKET

Every Friday morning, rain, shine, or flooding of the Cher, is market day in Montrichard. People come from kilometers around to wander the temporary stalls that take over two blocks in the middle of town. Armed with a basket that signifies we're not just any old tourists, but residents. albeit with a strange American accent, we walk down our now-familiar street into town.

Like natives, we choose the weekend's meals based on whatever happens to be in season. Chestnuts in fall, endives in winter, white asparagus in spring, bright red strawberries in summer. Advice is ours for the asking. Madame, the strawberry-seller offers a sample to gauge which of the eight varieties we might want. Every small box is priced differently. When my hand strays to a small box that's got the smallest price attached, Madame explains, "That one's best for *confiture.* You'll need to add sugar.*" She points to another three boxes away. "That's the one for dessert. Much sweeter." I'm reminded of my geraniums and our mattress, now convinced that from the largest to smallest purchase most French merchants work harder at <u>not</u> selling things. Or rather, they insist on discussing the merits of each purchase to ensure they've made the sale that will fit the buyer's need. Though it makes shopping a long-winded experience, it warms my heart. I begin wishing that the free enterprise system in the states had some of this socialist streak built in.

Half the shopping time is spent greeting friends or threading our way through groups of other people's friends who clog the narrow passage that's left in the street once the stands have been installed. The green and white awnings tilting out from the refrigerated cases come in handy on rainy days. We've acquired the ability to hop from one to the other. It's not as dry as in a supermarket, but it's a heckuva lot more fun. Besides, it doesn't matter if you become a bit humid

76

personally. The object on rainy days is to protect the baguette. I was in charge the day that started off nice, then caught us off guard with a fine drizzle. We had no protection for our crispy baguette. No umbrella. No rain jacket to tug around it. Not even a plastic bag to throw over the long end sticking out of the basket. We watched our crisp crust grow soggy and soften until the long stalk sticking out of my basket hung its head in shame.

Whatever the weather, American visitors are enthralled with the outdoor market. You'd think they'd never seen food before. Come to think of it, they haven't seen it like this. Their cameras come out to record the chickens hanging heads down, the chunks of fresh lamb, bins of briny mussels, snails and sardines. Their enthusiasm is catching, and reminds us of our own novice adventures before market day became our usual mode of shopping.

Every town of any size has its market day, which is invariable, rain, shine or very rarely snow. Locals can all tell you whose stall is set up in what town and in what location within that town on what day. Gradually we discovered our favorites. The olive man's stand is stationed up the hill, after the cross street, on the right. He fills his bins with plump black and green olives, each one stuffed or spiced with something different. Soaked in garlic or lemon or vinegar, filled with piquant peppers or almonds, they represent the French connoisseur's quest for the ultimate taste.

Just below his stand to the opposite side stands the petite Vietnamese woman with her French husband. She makes the excellent spring rolls that are layered behind the glass of a miniscule, wheeled cart. Directly across the aisle from them is the double-length bed of ice chips on which fish of every size, shape, and color lay tail to tail, glossy eyes gleaming. Down the line are found the barbecue chickens touted as free-range and the sausage-stuffed mushrooms that the man in the grease-stained white apron bastes to delicious richness under the barbecue drippings.

Then there's the man who makes *chevre* or goat cheese. Tall, tanned and lean of cheek like a young Clint Eastwood, he charms the women by smiling his way through every Friday morning. Even that wouldn't convince the fussy French housewife to purchase his wares, except that his cheeses are pure white, creamy, and available in varieties ranging from liquid to gently moist to dry and strongly aged. Just to prove how good our judgment is in selecting his cheese each Friday, he proudly displays the paper that announces his *chevre* won first prize at the nearby goat festival.

***

This particular day we have visitors from Atlanta. Of course, our garden is missing geraniums. Still too early. Our friends don't complain since they don't even notice. The only complaint is voiced by our caffeine-deprived friend, Tom.

Tom and his wife, Dale, John and I set off to explore the market and plan a feast for lunch. Tom was intrigued, of course. But he hasn't been in France long enough to lose either jet lag or his media rep mode. We had just reached the lower level of the market area when he asked where to get some coffee to go.

"We just had coffee at breakfast," I said.

"I like lots of coffee. 'Sides that was decaf. I want real coffee. I won't hold you guys up. I'll just get a plastic cup and bring it with me."

"You can't do that."

"Sure I can. I won't be long. Just point me in the direction of a take-out counter. I'll catch up with you."

"You can't."

"Sure, I can. I'll get a take-out."

"The coffee's there." I pointed toward a café. "Or there." I pointed to a temporary stand set up with small high tables and stools.

78

"But you can't get it to go. You can't eat and run here. You can't even drink and run. You have to sit down."

"Nah, I'll just get a plastic cup."

I shook my head.

"No plastic cups?"

"No plastic cups."

We gathered his wife, Dale, and John. We all sat and had coffee with Tom while the market swirled around us.

"It's kinda small, isn't it," Tom said. He poked at the miniscule cup with his index finger. He couldn't get it into the espresso-size handle.

"You can have a larger cup if you order a *grand* instead of just *un café*."

Tom sipped. "It's awfully strong," he grunted. I was beginning to wonder if we were about to start the guest visit from hell.

"Yes," we agreed. "It's strong but you become used to it."

He thought that one over. Tom ordered another espresso to try out the theory.

Finally we were ready to tackle the market aisles again. Now we were on track to lunch makings. Tom followed Dale, who was enthusing properly about the produce.

Except for Tom. In front of the bread stand, he mumbled, "This would be perfect if I could sip coffee as we walk." Beside the fishmonger, he said something about the backwardness of the French in not having coffee that travels.

Finally, on the walk back to the house, his entrepreneurial nature kicked in, "I could earn a fortune importing plastic cups."

***

In our narrow kitchen the four of us unloaded the basket. It was a bounty worthy of visitors. Crisp endive, radicchio, and bright red tomatoes. Three kinds of cheeses –

79

goat, St. Nectaire, and Camembert. A slab of hearty country pate. A small plastic bag of green olives, slippery with garlic-flavored olive oil plus a neat bag of small black Niçoise. A chicken, freshly grilled on the outdoor spit at the market, with sausage-stuffed mushrooms Monsieur had placed under the drippings. And, *un pain*, a large oval loaf of bread.

We laid the table outside with a blue calico cloth and picnic. Tom and Dale oohed and ahhed. We treated ourselves to wine, settled back and relaxed, enjoying the sun.

"Do you eat like this every day?" asked Dale.

"Not as much, but we eat as well, yes," we said, pleased that our guests were starting to relate to the simple joys we experience here in France.

Tom looked thoughtful. "You mean they don't even have take out cups in bigger cities?"

***

Two days later our friends left and I check my e-mail. One message is there, to be passed on to Dale. It's her boss from Atlanta, a maternal woman who asks how the trip's going. She ends with a word of warning to her employee.

I re-read the message and don't know whether to laugh or cry at the American impression of French food. "Be careful what you eat there," the woman warns, "The food isn't packaged or frozen or canned."

Right, I think, laughing. It's something called "fresh."

***

Six months later, we take a trip back to Atlanta. Dale repeats her thanks for our host and hostess-ing and repeats how much they'd enjoyed the trip to France. Then she adds. "Tom's complaining about the coffee."

"I know he didn't like it." I admit. "He made such a fuss at the market."

"No," she laughs. "Now he's complaining American coffee is too weak. He's making me add double the grounds."

Go figure.

***

In normal circumstances, when we've filled our basket with goodies at the market, we adjourn at noon to the local *Bar du Centre.* No take-out, just good company. The *Bar* is the gathering spot for a local group of English speakers who fill a small round table. We never know who will show up. But inevitably the group expands with new arrivals and friends of friends. (Our one visit with Tom and Dale solved the coffee problem since we ordered wine. Tom didn't complain. Though he *did* mention his preference for vodka.)

The chat comes in handy for people living in a foreign land. We discuss the best restaurants. What films are coming to the English-language theater. When the next party will take place. Wine is cheaper than the coffee *crème, l'eau minerale* or Coca-Cola. Nevertheless, the small glass of wine at that point was equivalent to 80 cents versus a dollar fifty for the Coke. If it's an effusive day, when someone has made a fortunate purchase of fresh mussels, one might celebrate with an extra glass of wine.

One day the group was celebrating, I'm sure, all packed together at three round plastic tables scrunched together. A British friend decided to deposit the morning's purchases in her car. She headed toward her nondescript silver gray Citroën. Like snow-white appliances that all look alike lined up at Darty, Starr's car looks like every other silver-gray Citroën, including ours. Starr calmly strode up to the car, opened the trunk, deposited her purchases, walked around to the driver's side, and noticed a strange package in the back seat of her car. That was fifteen seconds before she noticed an even stranger French man sitting behind the wheel. He said nothing, just looked bemused at the gift of groceries.

81

Starr calmly retraced her steps, opened the trunk, recovered her belongings, and retreated. Her matching Citroën was around the corner.

**

Our town's regular food shops are open more often than the Friday market but that's not saying much more. You can't count the days off, three-hour lunches, and various holidays. Since each store is small and independently-owned, les *proprietaires* set their hours to provide the family members who work there with their free time. Seven days a week, twenty-four hours a day is a concept that hasn't reached Montrichard.

One sizzling summer afternoon I set off for the automatic teller machine in town, passing a small butcher shop on the way. It was particularly amusing to see a sign on the window: "Out to the café around the corner." Obviously, *Monsieur* couldn't have been expected to handle a hot day like that without a mug of cold *pression.*

**

We discover that the French appetite for excellence is formidable. No detail is too small. When I request an avocado, Madame the vegetable clerk asks me when I want to eat it. "Today," I might say. "Lunch or dinner?" she'll insist.

Le chocolatier is my personal downfall. He's not Clint Eastwood like the *chevre* cheese merchant, but his wares are even more tempting. This paragon of calories won the French *Medaille d'Honeur* for excellence, a fact attested to with the kiss on both cheeks by Chirac and the proclamation high on the wall above the neat cellophane packs of crisp sugar cookies. Whether these *bisous* were appropriate or not between men was not the question. It just made it official.

We've enjoyed his triple chocolate tart (dark, milk and white), creamy éclairs and mouth-watering truffles dusted in cocoa to look like their namesakes, the mushrooms. But in the interest of solid and fattening research, we're gradually working our way through the dozens of other choices.

We want to ensure that the award was warranted.

***

Le chevaline is located beside the store where we purchased our mattress in our first throes of getting settled. We never paid much attention to it, probably because it was rather small and nondescript and we were more interested in getting bedding than hay. We did notice some pretty pictures of horses in the window but other than that we rushed by looking for more immediate needs than a poster for an equestrian show.

As John and I settled in we began to take in the town's finer details. We were passing on that side of the street and noticed two people in line at a glass counter. Something clicked. The counter appeared to be a butcher shop. Butcher shop. Horse pictures. "No, it couldn't be," we said to each other. "Yes, it could and is," Marie-France explained later.

I've still never entered the store, though I see people buying the rich red horse meat at the glass case. The line lengthened noticeably during the worst of the mad cow crises. "It's quite tasty," said Marie-France. "I have a recipe if you want it," she added.

We pride ourselves on being open-minded about trying new tastes, but in this case we nayed.

13
SUMMER OF THE ARTISTS

The local *Association des Artistes* has grand plans. They will convert our town square into their version of Montmartre, the hill-top square in Paris where painters gather before their easels and paint for the multitudes of tourists. Place Barthelemy Gilbert sits within a brochure-throw of the *Syndicat d'Initiative,* the town's Tourist Bureau, so visions of milling throngs with open wallets are dancing through the artists' heads. These *amateurs,* which in French simply means lovers of art, rather than the slightly derogatory English meaning, envisage themselves selling *tableaux* with wild abandon.

Never mind that tourists don't exactly throng through our town of 3,800 souls. It didn't bother the artists. If they never sold a painting, at least they would have reason to gather together, install their easels under the shady plane trees, and have a glass of wine.

The idea gathers steam. The mayor agrees that this was a fine idea. The event would add *animation* to the town in the summer and add a cachet of culture to the usual array of market produce. He would ban parking from the small square on Saturdays in July and August to make room for the artists. He would even support the event with an opening toast of champagne.

The event is to be called *L'été des Artistes* and the town hall will contribute posters to help promote this "Summer of the Artists."

John is as thrilled as the rest of the artists. He'd always envisioned himself with a beret. On the first Saturday, John gathers his easel, a prepared canvas for painting a scenic view of the square, and a few completed paintings that he'll prop around him to lend ambiance.

This first Saturday is the grand kick-off in more ways than one. We arrive in time to see a massive white horse who appears to be an unwilling participant in the event. The skittish beast is being led down an alley toward the square. Its regalia includes a black saddle and headpiece with crayon-colored yarn balls that bounce wildly about its ears. It would be enough to make anyone irritable. The horse is no exception. His head tosses. He snorts irritably. His hoofs flail and the crowd edges away.

Someone tells us that the horse belongs to a guest artist from southwest France who has been invited to perform for the opening ceremony. "Why a horse?" we ask. No one knows. Was it the artist's transportation from the southwest?

The crowd passes along the news that the special guest had studied with no less a personage than Salvator Dali. We're pretty sure they're talking about the artist, not the horse.

By noon, the crowd has grown to include the artists, their friends, townspeople and a few tourists who happen to be passing through. Everyone is milling about and growing restless. The event had been scheduled for ten. It's now after eleven. The horse is being paraded around the edges the square to dissipate extra energy, but every time he whinnies we hope he doesn't dissipate it with a kick through the crowd.

Our own energies are flagging. It's almost lunchtime and the special event is definitely lagging. We have no idea what is supposed to happen here, with a prancing horse. Suddenly, the choreography of the scene changes. Without any noticeable instruction people move to the edges of the square, leaving the center open. The horse has disappeared. For some reason, that's more unnerving. No one knows from what direction he might start kicking next.

From the far corner, an apparition appears. A tall, black-bearded man strides across the square, his black cape billowing around him like a roiling sea. As he reaches the center, he doffs his black hat with a flourish. Zorro apparently still lives.

Two buxom maidens prance behind him dressed in faux-Medieval gowns adopted by Renaissance fairs the world over. Behind them comes a young man in civilian duds, gingerly leading the missing white stallion, who is calmer but not enough to make those in the crowd near him feel good about it. It occurs to us that the horse's skittishness is just one problem with this particular participant. Like all dog-loving towns in France, we have our share of dogs and their evidence. We've managed to avoid most of it but today we vow to be especially vigilant.

Zorro's look-alike says something to Basile, then moves majestically to the center of the square, reviewing the proceedings like a general. Basile and two assistants appear from somewhere behind us, straining under the weight of a painter's canvas the size of a Mack truck. They prop it up near our end of the square, between two lofty plane trees. The horse neighs and pulls at the reins. The crowd near him moves back. Perhaps he's caught a glimpse of the horse meat store? The brave young man gives up the reins and one of the Renaissance maidens leads the horse away down the alley, calming him with sweet nothings.

Several minutes pass and Zorro works the crowd with bravado. The mayor uncorks champagne and his deputy pours as artists, friends, and the thirsty gather to take a glass. Ahh, but before we can drink, the mayor makes a speech. The assistant mayor makes a speech. The president of the Art Association makes a speech. Finally, the mayor proposes a toast and we are allowed to drink. We drink to avoiding horse doo-doo.

The plastic champagne flutes and empty champagne bottles are cleared from the center of the square. We can feel the crowd's anticipation – or hunger pangs. The time has come and gone with the prancings and the toastings. Let's get on with it, we want to scream. We're not proud of our American impatience. But we *are* hungry. To the left of us in *Les Truffeau*, our favorite café. The tables are all empty, just waiting to be filled. We intend to fill one of them soon.

Still, the event is intriguing. We have a man in a Zorro costume. Two maidens with a white horse dressed in yarn balls. And a white canvas the size of Mont Blanc.

The champagne helped to increase the crowd and we've lost sight of everything but the mountainous canvas. Suddenly, the crowd parts nervously at the sound of horseshoes, and, *voila*, Zorro appears, mounted on the horse. He trots toward the far corner of the canvas, pauses briefly to assess it, then kicks the horse forward. He reaches into a cloth bag in front of the saddle, raises his arm. Is that a white ball? He throws and releases. An egg filled with red paint splatters resoundingly on the upper right of the canvas. Legs of red like an octopus drip toward the pavement. Between the amazement, I wonder if the paint is acrylic and did Monsieur the Mayor know that his square would be under siege in exactly this way?

He wheels the stallion around the square and the crowd does an inadvertent version of the wave to increase the safety margin. Between each round, our Zorro-esque entertainer repeats the baseball throw with a yellow-filled egg, a blue-filled one, and a green. By now we're trying not to laugh. So is everyone else who has no idea what this Dali apprentice has up his sleeve. Other than a violet-filled egg, perhaps. Interesting, this act, but stressful as well. We must all not only give a wide berth to the horse but keep an eye on the egg trajectory.

We relax when the colored eggs are finished, Zorro dismounts, and the stallion disappears stage left to the alley. It's at this point that Zorro pulls the hilt of a sword from its scabbard.

At least we don't worry about this errant knight knifing us. The tip of his sword is a giant paintbrush. Zorro strides to the canvas and dips his sword/brush into a bucket of black paint. With swashbuckling moves he begins at the red splotch and gravely thrusts a line to the left. He swirls again. And again. A naked nymph appears with a single hip, a rounded breast and a rather shy face. The lines continue, creating an eagle on the upper left, as part of the yellow and blue blobs.

The painting completed, he bows to applause.

Amazingly, it's not bad. *Pas mal*, at all.

We adjourn several feet to our lunch table and discuss the painter and the painting with Basile. The painting will be dedicated to the town, which will keep it as a memento or sell it.

We never see it again.

***

The remaining Saturday art days are less dramatic. John, along with other members of the art association set up easels and tables and chairs in the square. They bring out watercolors, pastels, oils and acrylics. They range completed works of art around them for potential sale. They raise paintbrushes and drawing pencils. They squint at their canvases. They squint at their neighbor's canvases. They look at half-finished paintings, comment politely, and have coffee.

Mostly, they talk.

It's by this means that we accumulate a new group of friends in town. Pierre stops by with his wife, Christiane. They're both eager to learn English and immediately inform us of the fact. Before we can blurt out that we're not teachers, they inform us that they've already begun the lessons. Meanwhile, Pierre asks John if he likes to play *boules*. John has watched the sport, much like Italian *bocce*, for years from afar, each time we've visited France on vacation. He's stared at the stolid players as they hefted their steel balls, weighing each shot carefully. He's imagined himself in the center of the group, all eyes on him as he throws the perfect, arching shot to land at the small wooden ball that serves as a target. But, alas, he's like the ten-year-old who's never picked for a team, Even worse, his impatient wife always hustles him away, eager to actually do something on her vacation other than stand and watch the deliberately slow and careful decisions and measurements applied to the game. Before I can say a word, John quickly accepts the invitation to join the regular group on the next Thursday. I ask him how he's going to manage the French alone, without his chief translator, and hope he won't request that I show up. Mercifully for both of us, he declines and says he'll manage.

***

Lunch is vital in France. It's to be shared. So the wives, husbands, and friends join the artists. We settle at tables within view of the paintings and share lunch for two hours. Each painterly Saturday at 12:30 the artist chit-chat moves *en masse* from the center of the square to one of the cafés that surround it on three sides. One in particular had been a derelict building until spring. It had been the site of numerous previous restaurant incarnations. All failed. But this time magic happens. The new owners, Stephan and Eric, have can-do attitudes. Eric does the cooking. Stephan's in charge of the marketing. He offers Basile free coffee, then free wine. For all I know, free meals. The artists make the bistro their home away from *atelier*.

We join the group and order from the large menu board. The special is *moules/frites*...mussels and French fries. It's served with heaps of fresh cut bread used to sop up the creamy sauce. Someone orders a *pichet* of wine. Buying a pitcher of the local red is the smart drinker's choice in the French wine regions. After all, this stuff is straight from the vintner next door. Why pay for a special bottle, when it's the same and much cheaper in a pitcher?

The first day we lunch with the group, we're still Americans at heart. We look at our watches. It's one-thirty. The artists order coffee and chat. The easels and canvases sit hot and lonely in the afternoon sun, while we laze under the green and white striped awnings. We look at our watches at two o'clock and imagine that the group will soon get back to the reason we've gathered – painting. By the end of the summer we've acclimated and stay seated most of the afternoon.

Rarely is anything sold except the mussels and fries at the café.

14
CHEAP EATS

We can't remember exactly who spilled the beans about Le Pont Bois. We were at Bar du Centre drinking wine at the time, which could explain the memory lapse. Two couples among the several English-speaking friends mentioned that they would be leaving early. They're heading to Le Pont Bois for lunch.

"We've never heard of that restaurant." I say innocently, always ready to be enlightened on new taste treats.

Except for John's, the other faces at the table turn toward me as though I'd shouted a four-letter word in church.

"You've *never* been to Le Pont Bois?"

Geez, no, we hadn't. Hunger pangs are raging at the moment so I'm waiting for an invitation. "You need to reserve in advance," one person says.

"Probably doesn't fit our budget, then," I joke.

"All included, for something like $10, figuring exchange rate," he counters.

Surely I'd misheard "For *le plat*, the main dish?"

"For everything. It includes the wine, of course."

Apparently this tiny restaurant is run by a cheerful woman whose husband absconded several years ago. She filled the void with food. She didn't eat it herself. She started serving it, lunchtime only, in the form of home-cooked meals to knowledgeable locals who reserve in advance.

This topic was getting interesting but as is usual in large groups the subject had already moved on to the sad tale of the fish shop down the street that just went out of business.

Perhaps I looked like a child locked out of a candy store because the woman next to me whispers, "It's in the phone book."

***

I dial the number and the woman who answers is amazingly astute. I had only said one sentence when she decides that I'm not French. I request a reservation at noon but she responds, not with a request for my name and the number of diners, but an interrogation as to my location. "*Vous êtes de la region?*"

I assure her that, yes, I am from the area. A swift mental calculation (always swift when threatened with the possibility of not being able to dine like a glutton for a pittance) makes me add that we live in Montrichard. I throw in the name of our French tutor. Fortunately, my further investigations had unearthed the fact that *Madame,* the tutor, was an old friend of *Madame*, the chef.

Satisfied, the gatekeeper *Madame* allows me to make reservations.

***

En route, we discover why we had never noticed the restaurant before. It can't be found. We must have passed within several hundred yards three times before we begin to suspect that the red-roofed, white stone building before us is something other than a rough-hewn barn, tucked in the middle of the countryside, with nothing but cows and vineyards as company.

The only reason we finally investigate more closely is the accumulation of vehicles – four cars and five EDF (*Electricité de France*) trucks –parked on the packed-down earth beside an open shed to one side. Under the open roof of the shed resides an ancient *pressoir,* the spiraling equipment used to press grapes for wine. It isn't grape-gathering season so either this barn has cows that need powerful milking machines or we'd found our restaurant

What we thought was a deserted barn from the outside is a bright and cheery, dining space inside. The occupants of those six EDF trucks are gathered at a long community table to one side. A dozen or so individual tables are topped with gingham tablecloths, set with

91

cutlery and wine glasses, dishes of olives and pitchers of glistening red wine.

Madame welcomes us. We give the password, Knorr, and she nods toward a table for two. Now what? We don't have long to wonder. A young waitress delivers plates of small *amuses-bouches*, which mean to literally "amuse the mouth." These include small bites of pastry filled with meat or salmon and two platters, one heaped with a shredded carrot salad and potato salad and the other of thick slabs of sausages and *paté*.

We'd already gathered that we would get whatever Madame was serving that day but the waitress does ask if we preferred the main dish of fish, lamb, or beef.

Before we can dig in she proposes a *kir*, the traditional French *apéritif* combining cassis liqueur and white wine. She asks in such a way that we realize this is included in the price. *Oui*, we nod in unison, *pourquoi pas.*

The rosy combination of cassis and wine suffuses the room. Everyone seems convivial, relaxed, and clearly enjoying themselves better than in any four-star restaurant. The EDF workers gathered at the long table are already applying themselves diligently to the main course. We realize why there are so many of them. Based on French law, all workers must be supplied with lunch. But if the company doesn't have a cafeteria, or if the workers can't get there, as is the case for the electric workers on the road, they must receive a chit for lunch. The chit is worth the same amount. Coincidentally, Madame, the chef who runs the restaurant has chosen that amount for lunch, including wine, at *Le Pont Bois.*

We plunge on. The main courses arrive – a tender chunk of lamb in a creamy mushroom sauce for me. Fresh trout in a beurre blanc sauce for John. On the side are green beans and new potatoes drenched in butter, mounded in a bowl so they reach almost as high as the rims of the wine glasses. The wine glasses are filled. The pitcher on the table is bottomless. Despite our best efforts, we can't finish it because the hostess insists on replenishing it.

We find reserves of gluttony we didn't know we had. We refuse to pace ourselves and take seconds. This is not the stuff of a Michelin feast – teeny and continental -- it's fresh, delicious and plentiful French home cooking.

As we pause for a breath, the waitress asks "*Terminé?*" We nod *oui*, but wonder how we stacked up as customers. Did we eat too much? Did we eat too little? Nah, that wasn't the problem.

She scurries away with empty plates and returns with a platter of six cheeses, triangular, rectangular, and round, cinder-tinged, yellow-topped, and blue-veined, with more crusty bread sliced into the wooden basket.

We sip more wine with our cheese course and discuss its merits. Evidently, just a table wine served at will from a pitcher. Still, it's delicious. It couldn't hurt to ask about it.

The buzz of voices in the room intensifies from the EDF workers and the few civilian diners like us at the tables. People lean back in their seats, relaxing from the ordeal of this copious lunch. But if the troops have slowed down, none have actually surrendered.

When dessert arrives, the oohs and ahhs outweigh our few murmurs of dismay when Madame plops not just one platter on the table but three. Apparently, someone canceled a reservation today and there are, sadly, too many desserts. She's provided us with plump slices of cinnamon cake, homemade apple tart, and neat chocolate triangles.

As we nibble at the crumbs, the EDF workers march jovially out, tossing *au revoirs* to the remaining diners. Noting the empty pitchers of wine on the table, I wonder how they can possibly return to work this afternoon without a three-hour siesta. An even-more jolting thought is the idea that they will be returning to work with high-tension wires.

We vow to arrange any future electrical repairs prior to noon.

***

We finish the meal peacefully with thick, dark espresso in tiny cups. The room has quieted after the release of the EDF. Madame and the waitress sit at the other side of the room chatting with each other. Madame looks at the two of us, slumping totally satiated against our chairs and suggests a small *degust if* – a tiny glass of pear or peach liqueur to settle the stomach. We get the impression that she is in particularly good humor and glad to have two people who've shown inordinate pleasure in her meal. This small extra was not offered the EDF. Sure, they'd eaten well, but the novelty has worn off them. They take the meal as their due, whereas we novices have counted our blessings at each magnificent addition to *le repas*. If there's one thing a French chef, whether legendary Paul Bocuse or Madame of Le Pont Bois, appreciates, it's appreciation.

***

Now's our chance to ask about the wine we'd enjoyed.

"Could you tell us the name?" we ask Madame. "We'd like to see about buying some for our own *cave*."

"*Bien sûr*," she says. "I'll get the address." She disappears into the kitchen where we assume she'll jot down the name and address of the local vineyard. She might even have a business card from the vintner.

Five minutes later Madame crosses the dining area, grasping a bottle, which she presents to us. "I couldn't find a pencil," she explains. "But *l'etiquette*, the label, would give us all the information we needed. The name and the town where the wine can be found. We note the name Oisly on the label. Only when we insisted on butchering the pronunciation, did she patiently coach us and then explain that this was her son-in-law's vineyard.

94

In the interests of research and family harmony, we gladly accepted the business-card bottle. Which, I might emphasize, was a full one.

Business cards were never like this in the states.

15
A CORKING GOOD TIME

The real estate ads in the Loire Valley, after mentioning such minor details as the number of bedrooms and baths, list the *cave*. No self-respecting home in wine country would be without one. These *caves,* rather than being the object of a spelunker's exploration, provide the ideal temperature and humidity for storing one's liquid assets.

Red, white, rosé, and bubbly wines all profit from proper storage in a cool temperature. The constant temperature of 62 degrees within a Loire *cave* makes it the ideal repository. The cliffs of the Cher and Loire river valleys are replete with these holes in the ground just waiting to be filled. Undoubtedly God planned it that way, providing proper storage below ground for the delicious end product created from the vineyards above.

Our house was originally built over a cave big enough to drive a Mack truck through. The underpinnings were then sub-divided over the years by other owners into functional areas. Thus, we have a furnace cave, a workshop *cave*, and the most important, an honest-to-goodness wine *cave*.

When we first moved in, a sheet of black plastic, splotched gray by mildew, hung between the five-inch thick wooden door and the arched stone entrance. The door was arched, but not exactly to fit, so the plastic served as extra insulation. Practical, but a grimy entrance to wine nirvana. The *cave*'s stone walls were rough, irregular, and cool to the touch. The floor was dirt, littered with chunks of brick and damp cardboard boxes. In a few areas, the dirt was partially paved with ridges of what appeared to be curved green enamel that created a wave effect here and there. Most of it was smashed and dirt had taken over. At first we thought that someone had tried a ceramic design that failed. Brushing off the curved shapes, like archaeologists at an ancient tomb, we discovered that some creative individual had tiled the floor with wine bottles. Empty, of course.

Perhaps it never occurred to him that wine bottles are breakable when walked upon. Or perhaps he imbibed a bit too heavily and broke the bottles as he was storing them, and later decided to bury the broken pieces *in memoriam* on the field where they'd lost their useful lives.

A few unbroken bottles still remained buried in the dirt but most of them had long ago turned to shards. Normally, one does not enter a cave barefoot so this wasn't a grave concern. However, it didn't add to the appeal of the cool, damp space. This was the same space – as yet empty of any vintage whatsoever -- that made my husband's mouth water -- or wine -- to fill it.

The wine cave elicits a peculiar response in the male of the species. They must visit it periodically. Preferably with friends. Visitors are often lured to the depths of a house to enjoy a damp tour of the wine cave. It's one thing when the wine cave is as impressive as a vintner's. It's another when the cave is dug into a backyard hillock, fitted under the barn, or situated behind one low, head-banging entrance sheathed in moldy plastic, such as ours. The only purpose I can see for the tours is to compare the sizes of the metal or wood racks holding the wines.

Sure, occasionally someone will pull out a bottle, peering closely at a faded label and mention a particularly delightful wine or a rare vintage, while all present are expected to make gratifying murmurs of approval. You might think that the visitor would then be invited to partake of the wines thus showcased. Nope. Rarely does one get to taste this magnificence during the tour. No matter how fluidly local wines might flow above ground, the host's special wines remain in the cave to mature, an event which occurs so rarely as to be virtually unknown unless one deigns to impress an important visitor. President Chirac or the Pope perhaps.

We're guilty ourselves. It's the equivalent of buying a special shirt and "saving it for a good occasion" while the tee-shirts get worn every day.

In the Loire (and virtually all wine regions of France, for that matter), the actual wine served for daily consumption often comes from a filling station for wine, otherwise known as the wine *cooperative*. Growers send their orphan grapes to the co-op, where they are combined in a mix-n-match vintage, that is, in most cases, perfectly drinkable.

Our first visit to the wine co-op began with an impromptu find. John was cleaning out our wine cave and replacing the shattered bottle floor with real tile when he found a hulk of brown plastic that looked like a large economy-sized milk jug.

It was a wine container, fondly nicknamed a *cubie*. John opened its tidy screw-top to see what might have aged within. It was empty. But he heard the thin wail of a wine jug dying of thirst. We would provide.

Along Route 76, across the river from the magnificent chateau of Chenonceau, we'd seen a portent, a true sign from above. High atop an expansive beige metal building were emblazoned the words: *Francueil Cooperative du Vin*. We hadn't yet determined how to pronounce the name of the village with its unwieldy ending of 'cueil' but we certainly knew the word for wine.

We were already familiar with wine tastings in France from previous visit here. Signs along the road point the way to a *dégustation* or tasting. Visitors can sample wines before buying and most vintners are generous in pouring. But they provide an urn or a floor grate near the tasting counter so tasters can merely swish the liquid in their mouths, swallow a drop or two, then spit delicately or not so delicately, into the provided receptacle. Then they repeat the steps.

It seems like a terrible waste of good wine to me. However, those who avail themselves of the spitting method indubitably choose a better wine than I do. After politely swallowing all those sips, my fuzzy decisions tend to be based on the *eeny, meeny* method.

This particular day, we park on the large gravel apron in front of the building and entered a barn-like structure with a two-story high ceiling. To the left is a curving wooden bar stacked with a dozen or so small wine glasses. Five wine bottles in various stages of emptiness (or fullness if you're an optimist) are standing among the spills on the bar top.

Scattered around the large open room are displays, mostly stacks of wine cartons, with a bottle or two on top with its name and price or promotional appeal. A counter near the door holds a cash register where four people are gathered in a crooked line, some with wheeled carts filled to the brim with cartons of bottled wines, others with *cubietainers* such as the one John holds loosely in his hand.

Subtly gleaming in the twilight along the back wall, stands a series of stainless steel tanks the size of a mammoth and roughly the same shape. We step around a cart heaped with wine cartons to get closer. These monsters come complete an elephantine trunk in the form of a heavy-duty black hose that curls on the cement floor.

Several people are loitering around the open space. Most of them look like country folk, with rubber boots, dirt-stained jeans, and plaid shirts for older men, tee shirts for the younger ones. Women are in short supply. One sits in a glassed-in cubiecle at the far end and the other is a matron standing with a man at the tasting table. We edge closer to the tanks, where a young man wields the nozzle, filling a large *cubie* – a white plastic version of our brown one. I begin to wonder if we'd washed ours out well enough.

"Alcohol *does* kill germs, doesn't it?" I mutter.

John shrugs. He doesn't care.

The young man hands off the white *cubie* to a waiting customer and we hold our *cubie* toward him. He's dressed in rubber boots and jeans. Judging from the wine splashes, I understand the boots. He asks if we want wine.

"*Oui*," we say. I wonder if anyone with a cubie has ever said no.

The young man waits and watches. We wait and wonder why he isn't filling our *cubie* as he had the other customer's. Does he not like the looks of the brown container?

"Which one?" he asks."The Cabernet? The Côt? The Gamay?"

John and I look at each other. That's right, we realize. We have to know which one of these monster trunks to tap, don't we? The man nods toward the bar where by now an older man is tasting, though he doesn't seem to be tasting to purchase so much as simply availing himself with the opportunity.

We wander over and a rubber-booted man behind the bar points toward the half empty bottles. We can try whatever we want. We pour. We sip. We evidently have not yet become true wine connoisseurs so we decide on the Cabernet. It tastes as good as any of the others and, we rationalize, we recognize the name.

At that point we move back to the tanks. With about as much formality as the attendant at a service station, our clerk applies the nozzle to the opening on our *cubie* and wine guzzles in.

He tops up the container, bringing bright red wine to the very edge of the mouth, then screws the cap on and hands it to us. We now have our 'little brown jug' in molded plastic. At the cashier's desk, we steal the wine. Or rather, it feels as though we're doing so. By purchasing in bulk, *en vrac* as they say, our five-liter container of wine, cost approximately $1.25 a bottle. And we'd opted for the good stuff.

Winos of the world could hold their annual conference here and save a bundle. As it is, we plan to handle the duty ourselves.

Once home, I ask John if he's ready for lunch. No way. This man is on a mission. He can't leave that wine just sitting in its little jug. He has to try out his corker. The proper equipment being essential for bottling wine, one of the first things we bought when we made the offer on the house, even before a bed or kitchen supplies, is what I refer to with typical French preciseness as the cork putter-inner.

I don't know the name for it since I have yet to see it labeled, but the metal gizmo with its foot-long lever and green tripod legs is found in virtually every French hardware store. It squeezes the corks in a vise until they pop gently into the neck of the bottles, there to expand and protect the wine lovingly for as long as it takes to develop its flavor – or be drunk, whichever comes first.

John prepares the empty wine bottles and rinses them out. We'd collected these bottles through great personal sacrifice by buying wine and drinking it. He carefully fills each one, spilling red wine cheerfully on the oak table outside the wine cave. Then, comes the magic moment. He places a cork into the bottle, applies the bottle to the cork putter-inner and pulled the lever. Nothing happens. He presses harder. The cork won't fit.

Then John asks me to read the directions on the cork package which explains that the corks must be softened in warm water for ten minutes.

"Oh," says the wine connoisseur.

Ten minutes later he tries again. Gently and gracefully the cork slides into the bottle. John repeats the steps with the rest of the bottles and it starts his love affair with bottling wine. (It helps that the wine in the *cubie* never fits exactly into bottles. There's always the odd bit left. Naturally, the bottler has to finish off the leftovers to avoid wasting wine.)

***

The process so fascinated my twenty-something daughter on her first visit to *les parents* that she filled and corked three bottles to take home as souvenirs. Waiting for a next flight in Cincinnati, she made the acquaintance of a Milwaukee dentist who was a budding wine connoisseur. He offered her $20 for one of the souvenir bottles of our local brew, which, if you recall, cost roughly $1.25 each. Being an impoverished graduate student at the time, daughter accepted -- and immediately began to calculate the possibilities of an import business.

**

In November, our region, known as the Touraine, its main city of Tours, and satellite towns near and far, buzz with purple activity. The first wine of the season arrives to a grand celebration. Known as *Touraine Primeur,* the wine follows the same basic principle as the more well-marketed cousin, *Beaujolais Nouveau.* Both are the first young wines from the year's grapes. Mostly, it's an excuse for a region-wide party.

Overnight, our small town becomes a fairyland for Bacchus. The town's maintenance workers clog the main street on a Tuesday, our town's "day off" when most businesses are closed anyway. They thread white lights through the now skeletal plane trees and hang more of them on metal frames that arch over the main route through town. Five-foot high grape clusters hang from every streetlight. They were painted royal purple with lime green stems by members of the Art Association members. John did his share, though much as we study them later, we can't attribute any one cluster to his artistic style.

Shopkeepers participate with colorful window displays based on grapes, wine, and harvest motifs. Yarn-haired dummies are dressed in field gear as though raring to pick the vintage.

Tastings are the business of the day and night. They begin before the official weekend with tables set for Touraine Primeur in the super markets. Even our bank joins in, a festive addition to the otherwise staid atmosphere, which I applaud on one hand (the one with the wine glass in it) while the idea of the free-flowing wine wherever a clerk is handling my deposit causes a moment's unease.

That was just the start of the season. It culminates in the third weekend of November with the *Fête de Touraine Primeur*.

On Saturday, the weather is, to put it mildly, crisp. Long underwear is called for unless we make it to the town's wine caves quickly. These make our home's Mack-truck sized space look like a mere dent. A series of parallel caves, more like tunnels, really, are hollowed out directly under the fortified *donjon* on the cliff above. This is our first view of them, since they're opened only a few times during the year. The *Fête de Touraine Primeur* is one of them.

The cave walls are rough like ours at home, the tuffeau stone darkened by age and moisture. The humidity soaks into your bones when you first enter the caves. You can smell the dampness. It's quickly dispelled when your nose is in a wine glass.

Before entering, we push our way through the crowds to a wooden stand on the street that sells official souvenir wine glasses. At 10 francs, or about a dollar fifty, the glasses are a bottomless font of wine. We're free to fill it at any of the tasting stands. The lists on each of the three entrances to the tunnels shows that there are dozens of vintners ready to convince us that theirs will be the primo wine this year. A few food stands are listed as well, presumably to improve the odds that some of the people inside the caves will be able to walk out of them without staggering.

It's difficult to know where to start. Wine tasting stands line both sides of the main and two branch tunnels. Hundreds of glass-carrying people crowd in and start to make the rounds. (Could this possibly be where the phrase "to buy a round" might have originated?) The proximity of warm bodies and cold Touraine Primeur does much to make one forget the freezing cold outside.

At noon the crowd starts to dwindle. We can get closer to the mushroom stand to question the woman behind the wooden crates about the version she's selling called black death. She assures us they're not only edible but delicious. I can't make myself buy them but we discuss the package of dried *girolles*. A passing friend recommends them, and pauses to provide a simple pasta recipe for them. We buy them then head for the pastry stand. Hunger is encouraging us to taste the differences between a *tarte au chevre* and another tart made with potato.

We wander back to sample a certain *Touraine Primeur* we'd missed but notice that some of the wine stands are now not only empty of customers, but of anyone behind the counter. The wines have been left behind for visitors to taste while the representatives are among the missing. We check our watches and, yes, of course. It's one o'clock.

Even the wine tasting stops for a proper French lunch.

* * *

Sunday morning of the festival is reserved for more solemnity, the mass and procession of *les confreries*. The *confreries* have as their sole objective the edification of one specific food or drink. Each *confrerie* has its own distinctive form of dress.

Naturally, wine is represented by several *confreries.* The nearby *Monmousseau* wine caves have by far the largest group, as attested by dozens of men and women dressed in baggy orange velvet robes with amorphous orange and green hats that look like the berets that ate Cleveland.

Truth is, there's enough velvet in the combined *confrerie* crowd to cover three hundred fat Santa Clauses in splashy colors. Velvet headwear in shapes of fez, beret, Nehru-style squares, high triangles, and squat squash blossoms bob down the cobblestone street, past the butcher and the five bakeries, the sounds of the trumpet and drums proceeding them. Representative flags of each group wag happily above the crowds.

They march this way up the steep steps to the church that lords it over the town. We sneak up in time to get seats inside the mottled *tuffeau* stone church and pay our traditional franc to the beggars who have been encouraged at this time to stand outside church. It's good timing. Everyone is in a jovial mood during the wine festival and can't say no.

The *confreries* march down the aisle like living stained glass windows, a bright contrast against the mottled white stone walls.

The mass, from what I understand of the priest's sermon, is dedicated to the wine, the wine makers, and us, the wine drinkers. He thanks God for the harvest and for the fact that the maintenance workers have been able, this year finally, to raise the heat level in the damp church to a respectable level that sits just above freezing.

As the offering, a representative from each *confrerie* leaves his or her group and marches up a side aisle and down the center, presenting the priest with a sample. The smiling priest gracefully accepts champagne and three-packs of wine by the score along with baskets of paté and sardines.

The mass over, the *confreries* reverse their march in a joyous procession. By now, the heathens who weren't in church, but tasting the fruits which we had just thanked God for, are below us on the street level, along with the master of ceremonies. Each group of *confreries*, with its flag hoisted proudly, take their turn moving down the grand stone staircase while the master of ceremonies introduces them to the crowd.

There's the Monmousseau champagne, of course and other wines. I particularly like the marine blue costumes of one group. They had tied whimsical scarves around their necks and wore jaunty navy berets on their heads. As I take a picture on one jovial, round-faced gentleman, I make the mistake of complimenting him on the shiny gold ornament around his neck, which I call a 'fish.'

Quickly, he corrects me. It's not just a 'fish.' Truly, I'd insulted a member of the sardine *confrerie*.

The crowd pleasers, however, are the last two representatives: two sprightly teenage girls dressed in bright red outfits that look like maternity dresses for someone who carries a baby at knee level. Their heads are capped with green and matching green fringe circles their necks. The master-of ceremonies seems puzzled when they appear. The group isn't on his official list. Apparently, it's a last-minute entry to the parade. He confers with them briefly while the crowd waits patiently.

The girls giggle and explain something to him. He smiles and gravely nods before introducing them to the crowd and solving the puzzle.

The self-proclaimed strawberry *confrerie* has made its entrance.

16
CREME CARAMEL SOUP

1 'boite' sweetened condensed milk
3 eggs
½ bag coconut
20 sugar cubes
Skim milk
Water

Caramelize the sugar with a few teaspoons of sugar in a cake pan. Let cool. Combine the eggs and concentrated milk. Add the equivalent of the boite *in skim milk and half the* boite *in water. Mix well. Add the coconut. Mix well.*

Pour the mixture in the cake pan on top of the caramel. Place the cake pan in a bain-marie *(a larger pan partially filled with water) in a cold oven, and cook at 8 or 230 degrees centigrade for 45 minutes. Let cool in the* bain marie. *Cake can be prepared in advance.*

At Annick's dinner party, prior to Marie-France's kissing lesson, we had enjoyed a meltingly delicious dessert. Annick labeled it *Gateau au Caramel.* (She later admitted the recipe was originally another member of the local Art Association. Turned out the recipe was passed around so much that the originator could never be strictly determined.)

In any case, the dessert was a sleek version of *crème caramel* laced with coconut. It looked like a loaf cake but wobbled like tight Jello (though better tasting). The topping was caramelized butter and sugar, adding a sweet note to the thick custard. The guests all took seconds, even the sleekest, figure-watching ones among them. Annick raved that the dessert was simple to make. Even better, it could be prepared easily in advance. The two advantages impressed one novice cook. Me. I'd never been much for cooking when we lived in the states. I was too busy working fifty hours a week. Now, I determined to try Annick's recipe for Starr and Doug and other English-speaking friends nearby.

A week later Annick copied out the recipe. It didn't have many ingredients, which is my criteria for deciding how difficult a recipe is. Even a non-cooking American can manage this one. With taste buds salivating, I gathered together the meager ingredients and prepared to tackle my first thoroughly French desert, straight from the French woman's kitchen.

The recipe *was* simple. *If* you could read French handwriting. *If* you knew the metric system. And, *if* you knew the cooking secrets that every French woman has learned from her mother's knee.

My mother's knee was American. So was her handwriting.

French handwriting is not just written in another language. It's written the way school children learn it, bearing no relationship to the cursive learned in the United States.

It took an hour just to decipher the letter forms. Then came the translation. John, wanting another helping of the *crème caramel* with coconut, which he would devour if I made the recipe, repeatedly returned to the kitchen with our five-inch-thick French dictionary.

Despite a few misgivings, the recipe *did* look straightforward. The first step was to make a caramel sauce. How to do this wasn't explained.

This was one of those things every French woman knows just as an American knows how to boil eggs. I searched through three cookbooks to find out how to do it correctly. Burn some sugar? I could do that. I'm good at burning things.

I followed through, being sure to measure accurately. No quantity was given in the list for the skim milk and water. When I got to the actual directions though, the mystery was solved when I saw that it required a *boite* of milk and a half *boite* of water. This was easy since I recalled from my high school French thirty years past that a *boite* was a box. Ah hah! Milk in France comes in one-liter boxes. How convenient. That must be what Annick meant.

It didn't take long after that to put together the meager ingredients. The caramelized sugar coated the cake pan smoothly. John checked my progress periodically. The smell of caramelized sugar is rich, deep and has the drawing power of honey to bears -- and husbands.

I add the rest of the ingredients and put the cake pan into a larger one with water, the newly learnt technique of creating a French *bain-marie.*

I weave across the kitchen carefully balancing the swishing liquid-filled pans of water and lemon-yellow ingredients onto the oven's middle shelf. I know that the eggs in the mixture will, after forty-five minutes, turn this concoction to a rich golden *crême caramel* that will hold a spoon gently -- and even better, will slide down the throat, as did Annick's version, in gentle waves of cream.

Forty-five minutes later, when I pull the pan out to test it, the waves are hurricane strength.

Nothing has solidified.

My fluky oven is to blame. It's always too low in temperature. I must have misjudged so I leave the dessert in for another fifteen minutes.

I check again. It's still thin as baby formula.

I turn up the oven 50 degrees. Another twenty minutes goes by. Nothing. An hour passes.

I take the mixture out of the oven. John helps by tasting it. "Delicious," he says and helpfully adds, "But isn't it supposed to be thicker?"

We scoop it out with spoons.

***

It takes several days but finally, with prodding from John who wants the real dessert to work, I admit what happened to Annick.

"It cannot be. The recipe is simple."

I suggest that perhaps it was my oven.

"How long did you say it was in the oven?" she asked.

"Two hours and a half."

She shakes her head gravely. "*Impossible.*"

We go through the recipe one step at a time. Caramel, check. *Bain marie*. Double check. The *boite* of milk. Check. Until I comment how easy it was to just dump a liter box of milk in the recipe.

She looks at me aghast. "But the *boite* is a small can, the evaporated milk size - not a full *litre*."

I'd dosed the recipe with four times the amount of liquid required.

The story makes the rounds of our French friends and provides the entertainment at every future dinner party. My version of the recipe is called *soupe au crème caramel*.

***

The U.S. cookbooks that traveled across the ocean with us prove useless in France. I never before realized how many American recipes require at least one, and usually many more, items that are canned, boxed, or already partially-prepared. Those products don't exist here. Or they're so rare as to make finding them take longer than cooking, eating and cleaning up from it.

Converting cups to liters makes any attempt at cooking an exercise in higher mathematics. The easiest things to make are salads and soups, both of which enable me to substitute without the dire consequences encountered in my *crème caramel* episode. For a beginning cook, they're the easiest. So I become expert at throwing together ingredients into a combination that nearly always tastes edible.

Fortunately, my friend of the *bisous*, Marie-France, cooks well enough for the two of us. As our friendship ripened, she came to the door one day, donating a modest jar of quince *confiture*. We enjoyed it on a fresh *baguette* for breakfast. Many breakfasts. There were only two of us and quince *confiture* goes a long way. Over the months, Marie-France would provide additional *confiture*, based on whatever was in season. We weren't eating *confiture* fast enough but I kept adding jars to the refrigerator until we could get to them.

In late summer, the blackberries were ripening along the roads that John and I biked through the vineyards. This year there was a bumper crop. I'd already gathered a kilo or so on my last solo hunt several days earlier. But picking blackberries is a lovely excuse for a bike ride so I dialed Marie-France's number.

Would she like to make a foray to harvest blackberries? It was a lovely day. We'd get our exercise and load up on fruit to boot.

We biked west toward the *chateau* of Chenonceau, riding along the river path. We passed the fields of cows. The path was dirt and rutted so that it felt at times as though you were riding a bucking bronco, but it was more peaceful than riding along the tarmac road above. The path had one additional benefit. It was lined with fat bushes of blackberries that the people in cars along the roadside couldn't see.

A line of blackberry bushes towered over our heads. It was a good spot. We pulled plastic bags out of our bike baskets and started picking…and tasting…picking and tasting. We chose each precious morsel, picking only the plumpest, juiciest berries, avoiding the thorny bits and the flat-headed spear-shaped bugs that liked them. I tried to remember when in my suburban, working life I had ever found such simple pleasure as a beautiful day and fruit, literally, of the earth.

It was a bountiful harvest. So bountiful that a half hour later I begin to realize that John and I already have more than enough blackberries at home for our needs. I know Marie-France loves to make *confiture*. So when we start to stow the bags of purple fruit carefully in bike bags, I hand my harvest to Marie-France.

At first she doesn't want to take it, but I explain that we have more than enough berries at home already, which we would have as a fruit salad. It has been fun picking but I want her to have them. No strings attached.

A day later Marie-France appears at our door. "I am on my way to town but I brought you this," she says. "*Voila.*" She thrusts three jars of homemade blackberry *confiture* at me. As I open the refrigerator doors, I look at the previous Marie-France gifts. The original quince jelly is gone by now. But it's been replaced by another jar. Plus apricot. Plum *confiture*. Strawberry. I add the three new jars and count.

There are nine jars of jam on the shelf.

***

We are leaving for a short trip but our garden is celebrating its last hurrah. Tomatoes are ripening quickly and they're succulent and sweet, fresh from the vine. It would be a shame to let them fall to the snails and the slugs. I give Marie-France and Michel the key to our gate and tell them to harvest whatever they want as the tomatoes ripen.

The rhubarb is already ripe for the picking so I gather that up, place the stalks in a bag, and as we leave town we drive by Marie-France and Michel's house, still shuttered in the early morning light, and leave it on their door handle

Two weeks later we return home, planning to straighten up the house, go to market, and be ready to greet family members arriving the next day. The phone rings while I'm pulling clothes from the suitcases. It's Marie-France.

"Your family arrives tomorrow."

"You remembered." I am impressed since my own memory for details is closer to that of a *passoir*, a sieve.

"Of course," she says matter-of-factly. "I'll be over this afternoon."

I don't ask why and continue the business of organizing the house for visitors.

Marie-France arrives mid-afternoon at the gate. After the greeting *bisous*, at which she no longer giggles, showing my progress, she thrusts a foil-wrapped oval at me. I look at her puzzled.

"It's a tart...I added a few apples to your rhubarb and made it last week and froze it. But it's fresh-baked this morning so you'll have dessert for your guests."

"But, but, but...Marie-France the rhubarb was for you and Michel."

"It was yours," she says.

I don't mention that the apples, crust, sugar, and time were all *hers.* She looks surprised that I would say anything. Doesn't everyone take a food gift, transform it into baked goods, and give it back?

A plastic bag is dangling from her wrist. Suddenly remembering it, Marie-France reaches inside and pulls out a glass jelly jar.

"Oh, and here's some more *confiture*. My neighbor gave me quince."

I'm beginning to realize that no matter what I give Marie-France it's simply raw material for her kitchen. A boomerang that always comes back. But in this case, it comes back sugared, canned, baked, or wrapped in a crust and ready to eat.

When Marie-France leaves, I deposit the new jar of quince *confiture* on the shelf that's now dedicated to Marie-France's culinary skills. Despite smothering our baguette every morning, I count ten jars of jelly.

17
PAY NOW...OR PAY LATER

Our road-weary *Citroën* is flashing its distress on the dash panel, indicating it's thirsty for oil. There are two different oil lights, however, and one shows that all is well. We head for the *Citroën* dealer outside town and request assistance.

Monsieur, the service manager, bustles out the door. A white lab coat flaps around his short legs as they pump toward us in efficient piston motion.

Jacky, as the blue-bordered name tag on his pocket announces, opens the hood and checks the oil. He jumps into the driver's seat, starts the car, and regards the offending light. He says something in rapid-fire French. John and I stare blankly. He repeats it, more slowly. We stare just as blankly.

He opens the hood and we play charades. Jacky points to cylinders and hoses. We guess at what they are.

Twenty minutes later we figure out that the car needs to be topped off with oil. But the car might have a slight leak. If the light comes on again, come back and Jacky will investigate further.

"*C'est combien?*" I ask how much we owe.

"*Rien.*" Nothing.

I'm sure I'd heard right. He'd spent ten minutes checking out the vehicle, twenty minutes explaining to mechanically and language-deficient Americans, and he'd topped off the oil. And he isn't charging us anything? We aren't even regular customers.

Ahhh, but we would be.

***

We are returning from a wine foray that had taken us to Saumur to stock up on the excellent red *Saumer Champigny.* The *Citroën* stops at a traffic light just as it's getting dark and a man in car beside us points out that one brake light isn't working. This, he reminds us, will be a *problème* if *les gendarmes* see us tonight.

We drive very carefully, on the way home and hope the gendarmes are busy with more important duties, such as dinner. The very next morning we take the car back to the *Citroën* dealer.

We pull up to the garage door. Jacky trots out again like a one-man pit crew. His white jacket is unbuttoned today and it flies like Superman behind him. John points to the rear of the car and taps the brake light.

"Hmm," Jacky says. We lose the rest.

We expect he will take the car inside and have one of his servicemen perform brake light surgery. No, this is to be a field job.

Jacky pokes around in the trunk to check the wiring.

"Ah-ha," he says.

Jacky trots back inside the garage and returns briskly with another piece of wire. He performs a simple operation, reattaching a vital part. *Eh voila*, the light works.

"*C'est combien?*" I ask, reaching for my wallet. Of course, this time there would be a charge.

"*Rien.*" Nothing

So far we are batting a thousand. This car with its mega kilometers isn't costing a thing. As non-mechanics, John and I congratulate ourselves on having chosen this used car well.

At least we did for five weeks.

***

The dream goes bust with a loud rattling sound that reverberates even more loudly in our town's narrow cobblestone streets. The muffler is *fini*.

This one couldn't possibly be a freebie. But we take the car in and Jackie once more reviews the situation. We get an estimate. That will be fine, we agree. Go ahead and fix it.

"*Bien sûr*," says Jacky. "Bring the car back on Thursday."

The new muffler purrs gently. At the cashier we mention that, by the way, the car needs a tune-up.

"We're busy now, bring it in three days," says Jacky.

We could do that. I open my wallet to finish the muffler transaction.

"*C'est combien?*" I ask.

"*Rien.*" Nothing.

We are beginning to like this service station.

"Well, nothing now," Jacky explains. "You'll be bringing the car for a tune-up. We'll straighten it all out then."

We bring the car for the tune-up just before we are planning a visit to the states so we ask Jacky if we can leave the car at the service garage. He can take his time with the tune-up. (We also rationalize that the station's fenced lot is a safer place to leave the car for three weeks than the street in front of our house.)

"*C'est combien?*" We ask, ready to pay before leaving on the trip.

"*Rien.*" Nothing.

"You're going to leave the car for the tune-up while you're gone on vacation. Just pay when you get back."

"We'll be gone three weeks," I remind Jacky, sure he wouldn't want two people who could be total deadbeats to take off without paying.

"*Pas de problème,*" he says. "The tune-up will be done then. Pay me later."

Of course, John, commented. Jacky *did* have our car.

The system, however, takes some adjustment for us Americans. We were raised on free enterprise, capitalism, pay as you go.

It's shocking to think that people anywhere could refuse to calculate every service based on immediate gain. It isn't, you see, just the service station that provides services without expecting an

116

immediate payout. From electrician to plumber to plasterer, French workers keep refusing to let us pay them.

"I'll send you a bill," says the electrician.

It arrives four months later.

Not for them, going out to the truck, presenting the bill and expecting the moola. Serious deadbeats could be happy for years.

18
THE LAMB FETE

It's July and the television news is reporting on the traffic, much as we would have seen it during rush hours in the States. Except that this traffic report depicts snaking red lines of *les embouteillages* as traffic jams weave south from Paris. French workers are stuffing their Renaults, Citroëns, and Peugeots onto the *Autoroute du Soleil* in order to find their sandy spot in the sun. As we watch the traffic reports, I wonder why some of those people don't simply wait for another day. It recalls to mind the time years ago when we first met Valerie, then a French exchange student. She joined us in June on a beautiful white sand beach in South Carolina. People were walking along the shore. Some had blankets scattered here and there. But Valerie wasn't at ease. Not at all. Finally, I asked what was wrong.

"There's no one here. Don't Americans like the beach?" she asked.

We couldn't convince her that, yes, of course, Americans like the beach but we didn't pack our vacation time so tightly that everyone takes their monthly vacations within the same two months of July and August.

"But how sad. It's so quiet."

The charm of this mass migration is exactly what we wanted away from. But Europeans in general, and the French in particular, enjoy vacationing *en masse* so they'll have bustling cafés, friends to chat with, music to hear. Anything less would make the beach very unbeachy and ruin *les vacances*.

Not to us. We're Americans and we're retired and we're not budging from Montrichard. The *triste* coat of winter has been shed with the advent of our own tourists. The tour boat plies the river Cher from Chenonceau to St. Aignan with its load of gawkers who see châteaux at each end of the trip. General activity is multiplied a hundred-fold. Every day a new sporting event, concert or gallery show is posted onto the windows of the *boulangerie, pharmacie* and, the bars. The latter have the most rectangular squares, which makes sense since those sitting around their *café, vin* or *pression* ---or all three if one decides to make a day of it – has to have entertainment.

The posters serve as conversation starters. It's amazing, the creative ways that the French find to celebrate something, anything. Concerts cover jazz (highly popular), classical, rock, and be-bop. Festivals cover all the basic food groups and then some. We note the coming strawberry *fête*, bread *fête*, stuffed tomato *fête, rillons* (a specialty of the region which is like barbeque without the sauce) *fête*, snail *fête*, and a *Fête de Moules*. We're attracted to the mussel festival because it's nearby, it's a beautiful day, and we can bike there. We peddle the flat road leading along the river Cher, but then we have to head away from the river, taking the hill up to St. Julien. Our legs strain and we're getting mighty warm. We're almost to the small town when a fact hits us both at the same time: we're not exactly seaside in the *centre* of France. Not only that, it's definitely steamy outside.

"Did you ever hear that old saying to only eat oysters in months with an "r"? I ask John.

"It's because they don't keep well in the hot summer."

"Aren't mussels like oysters? They have shells. They come from the sea."

My husband considers this as logical. As we slow into a lower gear to get up the final crest of the hill, we're doubled over our bikes. Rather in the same position, I think, as we would be if we ate the odd bad mussel.

We can't make it all the way up the hill anyway so we wimp out and walk the bikes. We're still trying to figure out why there would be a mussel festival in the middle of the summer in an inland village. A few cars drive past us as we walk. We crest the hill and hear a band playing not too far off but it's hidden behind trees and walls.

119

People seem to be heading in the direction of a small church in the hamlet, but disappear into a gate at the corner of a two-story building. We shrug, lock the bikes to a tree, and follow them. All the time, we're deciding that we can look. We don't have to eat anything in a shell that could cause July-doesn't-have-an-r-in-it-and-we-told-you-so incapacitation.

The field apparently belongs to the school building that shadows it on the left. On the other side of the field, rows of portable tables and benches create a dining area, with a ceiling of canvas. More tables are arranged in a long line to the right of that section, creating a serving bar, behind which middle-aged women and men are bustling about, taking cash and serving beverages in return. Wine bottles are being tipped up to fill small juice glasses. Some people are taking entire bottles back to the tables. A small blackboard at the back of the enclosure lists the prices. Eighty cents buys the small glass of wine. You get the entire bottle for $3.50. No wonder the serving crew is having trouble keeping up. At the far end, some of them are arranging paper plates for the main dish. The possibly offending *moules* are sitting in huge stainless steel bins, and some of them are already being served to early diners. Their accompaniments, French fries, are crisping up nicely in the hot oil.

We look around at the entrance. People are still streaming in. This hamlet isn't that large, but apparently everyone is here. Plus some. We, ourselves, aren't from the village but we see enough people in large groups of all ages that it's evident these people are local.

We rationalize that if whole families from the village turn out, can the village fathers really be planning mass poisoning by mussel? We discover they've been doing this festival for years and assume they must know something about what they're doing. After all, a few deaths here and there might have given them pause to question that r-in-the-month rule.

120

We bravely dig into a bowlful of *moules* with matching potato *frites*. The wine washes it down well and we don't feel sick at all. We go back for seconds.

***

We're already becoming jaded by the abundance of *fêtes*. We can't handle them all so it will be necessary to pick and choose. But how to know which ones are worth our efforts? We don't want to waste a Saturday at just any old festival when we could be at a better one just down the road. Then someone in Friday morning's post-market crowd happens to mention the *Fête du Mouton* – the Lamb Festival. Now that's something we can really appreciate. And we don't have to worry about eating it in a month without an 'r' either.

We drive toward Pontlevoy and the good vibes start when we're still two blocks from the destination. We become part of a trail of cars creating a mini *embouteillage* on what appears to be a narrow farm road leading to nowhere in particular. People are strolling from town along the edges of the road. Around the corner cars are multiplying row upon row in a field up ahead, an improvised parking lot sans asphalt. Just to our left a narrow line of poplars casts shadows and some independent and smarter souls are turning before reaching the field. We see the point. We congratulate ourselves on installing our car there, in the shade.

We pass a carousel for children but we sense more than little lambs as soon as we enter. Straight ahead pens of sheep give off the gentle odor of manure. We considered visiting this agricultural exhibit but one sheep looks the same as another to us. Unless it's cooked. Thinking about it, perhaps it's better to *not* think about it. We turn around and head the other direction where we'd seen smoke rising.

As at the mussel festival, the lamb stands are created from folding tables and canvas tops. But there are more of them in order to accommodate the large crowds that are already elbow-to-elbow at the wine bar and stacked at least thirty deep in two lines leading to the

121

food counter. Obviously lamb is more popular than mussels in July. At one side, a woman collected cash and provided a chit to be used at the stand to collect the meal. The choices were a lamb kabob and fries or the more complete, four-course *mechoui* meal. *Mechoui* is a word we've never encountered but we find out that it's a barbecue and we wander over to see whole lambs being roasted. A delicious, sweetly char-grilled aroma is wafting over the heads of the crowds. Men in full aprons intently slice and heap grilled meat onto huge platters. Other men pass the heaping plates to the women at the improvised counters who add meat to cardboard plates, the kind that are nicely divided in various sections. Each section has its filling: salad, a slice of lamb, French fries, a piece of cheese, a hunk of baguette, a slice of something that looks like a fruit cobbler. Just a little of each, but everything's there for a four-course French picnic. All that's missing is the wine. That's easily fixed. One of us stands in the line for the food, the other in the wine line and then we'll meet at the dining area where we've already seen some friends at a long picnic table. (I'm food, John's wine and he's done faster. That means either a) the lamb was more popular or, b) more likely from the bottles heaped on every picnic table, the wine is considered more vital and thus more attendants have been dedicated to the liquid refreshment.)

The English-speaking group is already seated. There are a dozen or so people, plus Starr and Doug's personal garbage disposal, Florence. I don't know how their golden lab can remain so calm with the tantalizing smells coming from the table but she's been here before and is sitting patiently, knowing that the tidbits will drift down from above. As we stuff ourselves with the perfectly grilled meat, I think about the lambs we'd seen in their pens for show. Ummm, they *were* for show, weren't they? I mean this isn't…

If I were to ever to become vegetarian that's the closest I'll come.

***

But no, the lambs we'd seen weren't dinner. They were part of the show, with the stars being a series of sheep dogs. This is one festival that wasn't merely for eating but for judging the mutts who come from all over France to compete on their sheep doggy merits.

We swig down the last of the wine. Ok, so it's the last of four bottles of wine that had somehow accumulated on the long table in the course of the meal. (Each of the men wandered off at some point to stand at the wine stand, thus contributing to the general well being.)

The shepherding competition is about to start. We head past stands filled with hand-knitted wool sweaters, lamb rugs, tiny lamb sculptures covered with real wool, and jellies. Not lamb, we presume.

Under the trees ahead a swirling mass of white cloud appears to be drifting across the grass. On closer inspection we see the sheep, being buzzed by a dive-bombing dog that scoots after them, adroitly nipping at any laggard's legs. The group is veering to the left, around the park's tennis court. The viewers stroll, keeping the sheep and the dog in sight.

The dog is the star, the sheep are merely bit players. He's stealing the show with glee, whipping back and forth, keeping the herd intact. He's so fast that it appears as though he knows when a sheep will try to make a break for it before the sheep does. Sure we love our little Folly, but disloyal as I feel, that sheepdog has to be the world's smartest *chien*.

But look! There's a gate up ahead. The sheep are in a rounded mass, all going toward it but obviously there are far too many to go through it together. The shepherd, who to this point has been offstage, shouts something to the dog. We can't understand the commands from this distance but he's insistent. The tension mounts. The true test is about to begin. That's the point of this exercise – literally, since the various gates and obstructions test the mettle of the dogs.

The dog darts from one side of the heaving mass of wool to another, first to the front, then back to the rear. Return to the front. Lay down quickly, allowing the sheep to slow. Then back to the side. Get those wandering fools in line. Back to the *other* side. They're getting closer. The first two sheep are through the gate. Will he do it? The wooly group is expanding at the rear. The next three sheep go through but two sheep have broken away on the far right side. The dog sees them and it's nip and tuck all the way.

But, while he's on the right, a sheep on the left straggles off. A sigh breaks through the crowd. He's got the rest of the herd through but the three wanderers are already well past the gate. It's too late to turn them back. Or is it? The dog heads for them and leaves the rest of the herd to slow down and nibble grass. The recalcitrant sheep don't get the rest. They're herded back around and through.

The performance continues behind the tennis court, where a car drives slowly by the sheep and the dog keeps them under control. Then he herds them into a pen and out again. He loses one who doesn't want to enter the pen. Though we don't understand the intricacies of the scoring we realize this was not a neat job and he's lost points. We're impressed anyway. But three dogs later, even more so, when one faultless performance is awe-inspiring. We now have a favorite to root for and consider ourselves sheep dog groupies.

As we exit past the sheep pens, we think of next year's shish-kebob.

19
A PRICK IN TIME

Some good friends will be vacationing in Italy for several weeks. Their tour company provides a two-bedroom villa, so although they can't get to France to see us, they invite us to join them there. It's an offer too good to pass up. Great friends, Italian countryside, wine, and a free place to stay.

But Italy, despite its close proximity to France, does not share the French love for dogs. We would have trouble finding accommodations on the drive over and back, much less restaurants, that would let our buddy travel with us. For ten days Folly would maintain his French residency without us.

None of us feels happy about this situation. Especially Folly. In the states he had shivered like furry white Jello the minute we took him to the kennel. He'd whine, paw at our legs, and try to climb into our arms. We felt like parents abandoning an infant. It wasn't even that the kennel was bad. The one we used in Atlanta had at one time saved his life, quite literally. It was clean, efficient, and staffed by gentle, dog lovers. Granted, the offices were shiny white tile with bright stainless steel tables, giving them all the warmth of a research lab.

That changed in the Loire.

We asked the veterinarians in Montrichard if they could recommend a kennel. We asked new friends with dogs. *Le chenil* they all named was called *St. François d'Assise* – because dear old St. Francis of Assisi was the patron saint of animals.

Despite the halo effect, we wanted to check the place out in advance. So off we go for a get-acquainted visit. All the way there, Folly wears a silly grin, his head bobbing out the window of our trusty gray Citroën. We follow the map north of Montrichard, through broad wheat and sunflower fields. We turn left at an old barn, then right at a faded sign. We chatter down a track dug between two open fields, following the roughly parallel ruts created by previous visitors.

Ahead of us a high wooden gate blocks the path. On the right is a barn, with a flat apron of dirt beside it. We park and get out to investigate. Folly jumps from the car and follows his nose to investigate whatever interesting smells he can find.

We peer through an iron-grated door to the right of the high gate. Inside, a grassy courtyard appears to be fully enclosed on all sides. On the left stands a stone house with blue painted shutters and a climbing rose trellis. Straight ahead is an ancient metal utility building. To the right is a longer, barn-like structure made of fieldstone. No white tile in sight and it's difficult to imagine a stainless steel table within miles.

We ring a doorbell attached to a speaker. The device erupts with static-filled French. "*J'arrive*," says a harried female voice.

Five minutes later the owner of the voice (and we assume, the kennel) strides purposefully across the courtyard in green gardening boots.

"*Bonjour*," she says. Folly stretches his neck to peek curiously through the grate.

"*Bonjour*," we say and introduce ourselves as the Knorrs and Folly. She introduces herself as Nadia Moreau. We are new in the area and we had made an appointment to visit the kennel.

"*Oui, bien sûr.*" Nadia bends to find a key beside the gate and opens it.

As soon as we enter the enclave we lose our dog. Not literally, because as we'd suspected, the large courtyard is totally enclosed. But the minute Folly is off his leash, he zooms away. He races from one grassy corner to the next, sniffing at a rock here, a bush there, grinning that wide doggy grin that says he's incredibly glad to be alive. He checks up on us periodically by zooming by like a Nascar racer, makes a tight loop, then speeds off to the far corners again in whirling, doggy glee.

On one pass, when he slows to thirty miles per hour, Nadia scoops him up in her arms. She snuggles him and kisses his white forehead, leaving a perfect lipstick imprint of red lips.

She sets him down, leaving Folly to his explorations and indicates that we should follow her to an annex to the left of the house. The office there holds a scarred wooden desk, two folding metal chairs, and six fluffy angora kittens.

We're invited to sit and be imprinted with the various rules and regulations. Nadia hands us the list of hours for drop-off and pick-up -- hours which, she emphasizes, must be strictly adhered to – and the requirements for making reservations. With us she is a stern headmistress speaking to the freshmen who are being warned to behave. Where is the smiling woman who had marked our dog's forehead with her passionate red kiss?

Finally, Nadia requests Folly's *carnet de santé.*

"What's that?" I ask.

"It is the record of his shots. He must have it, of course."

"Of course." I produce the shot records from the states, in English, of course. But it had worked for immigration when he entered France.

"*Non, non.* He must have *le carnet de santé.*"

Folly would need an official French record of his shots. His entire health, in fact, would be recorded in a passport-sized notebook. This is France and every dog (and human, by the way) has a *carnet* to keep the health records in one place. Nadia explains that it is essential to Folly's continuing health and agility in chasing birds and lizards.

I try explaining that he isn't a French poodle, not even a French mutt, but Nadia stands her ground. Folly cannot stay at *St. François d'Assise* kennel unless his records are written in an official French *carnet de santé*. We look outside and see the little guy grinning and sniffing. He likes this place. He actually likes it!

We promise the *carnet*.

The next morning Folly and I stroll through town to *les vétérinaires*. The office is situated just behind the 15th century medieval wall, in a renovated 19th century *maison*. The reception room is strictly utilitarian, with black and white checkerboard tiles and a wooden counter. The shelves in the background hold the *medicaments* necessary to fight French fleas, worms, and doggy heart disease.

Three people are working behind the counter. A rough guess assumes that the *Monsieur* in the knee-length white cotton coat, reminiscent of Jacky's at the *Citroën* dealership, is the veterinarian. He's flanked by two women, one a dour brunette of sturdy stature and middle years. The other is a slightly built, pink-shirted young woman in her early twenties.

I take a deep breath and begin composing my French explanation of what we need. I speak to the middle-aged woman but soon I've captured the attention of all three people behind the counter.

Apparently, this is a slow day for veterinarians in a small country town, because as I get to the problem of the *carnet* a second man appears in a white coat. My accent makes them an eager audience. I am news, I suppose. Or, rather Folly is. One admires my little guy and asks what he was.

"He's a mongrel from the pound," I say. "He's American."

That particular American is looking distinctly unhappy at the medicinal smells and the glimpse of steel table through the swinging door.

Meanwhile it becomes apparent that the *carnet* situation is complicated. American dogs don't have *carnets*. But Nadia at the kennel – they nod, they know Nadia, of course – needs to have the *carnet* so Folly can board there.

The first veterinarian explains that Folly would get a *carnet* when he had his inoculations. *Pas de problème*. Four heads bob up and down in sequence. This is simple. This is *normale*. This is all perfectly logical.

"But," I say, "Folly has already had all his shots in the states. He doesn't need them before we have to leave him at the kennel."

Four faces grow grave. Ahh, this is the crux of the *problème*. They are accustomed to French dogs who grow up in the system. How should they handle this, when the American dog has no French history?

Finally, one vet decides to be an innovator. Do I have an international certificate to show that Folly had had the required shots?

"Certainement, but Nadia at the kennel insists that he needs an official *carnet*."

This generates more bobbing heads and enthusiastic suggestions as each person, veterinarian one, veterinarian two, dour receptionist and cheerful young assistant makes his or her contribution to the discussion. This is true French *equalité* in action.

As usual, the French adore any discussion and *un problème* brings out the best of their rapid-fire French. At one point the junior woman in the group holds forth for several breathless minutes of explanations and recommendations while the two veterinarians and the older woman listen intently. Then they add their comments. I can't resist adding that she is very enthusiastic. She smiles.

But all I want is the small booklet called a *carnet* with Folly's shots listed in it.

I pick up Folly to bring him closer to the counter in order to engender more sympathy for the cause. Each of the four admire my dear little mongrel profusely, then continue with their attempt, very serious and very French in nature, to solve the problem. What to do? The kennel needs a *carnet*. Folly doesn't get a *carnet* unless he got his shots. But he doesn't need shots. He's already had them.

Couldn't the information just be copied into a *carnet*? I ask.

This seems a novel thought. No one responds.

Finally, the young woman suggests that we add someone else to the discussion. The person who had initiated *le problème*. They would call Nadia at the kennel.

Why not? I think. This simple task is turning out to be so complicated we might as well make it a six-way conversation.

After more discussion on the theme of what we'd been discussing for the past twenty minutes, it's determined that Nadia would, after all, accept the international health certificate.

I sigh in relief. It's getting towards noon and I'm ready to go home to lunch. The four heads across the counter might have been thinking the same thing. They turn to me as one. Where is the certificate?

In my nervous French explanation, all I had shown the vets was a bill for the shots. It lists what Folly had received in the states. Where is the actual international certificate? I couldn't remember.

"But," one vet prods, "you had it in order to enter France with your dog."

"Well, not actually. No one at the *douane* asked for it."

That didn't raise any eyebrows. Apparently the customs officials have been lax before.

Finally, I remember the certificate is in the glove box in the car, left there after the kennel visit. I run back and retrieve it and wave it victoriously before the review stand across the counter. After close inspection by eight eyes, all agree it is *"parfait."* Folly is completely *regulaire*.

I say *"merci"* and prepare to leave.

The dour receptionist stops me. *"Attendez,"* she orders. What now?

She opens a drawer behind the counter and produces a small square folder in blue plastic. It isn't the *carnet* itself. It's the cover.

130

"How do you call the dog?" The first vet asks.

The receptionist produces a large marker and smiles. She hands it to the vet with the precision of an operating room nurse to a surgeon.

Monsieur, le veterinaire, prints "Folly" officially in capital letters on the front cover as I spell it out. Then he asks for all the papers from the states that had been passed back and forth for discussion. He places them neatly inside, closes the cover, and hands it over.

"You will get the *carnet* the next time he needs shots," he says.

Five people and one small dog bid "*au revoir*" with handshakes and paw shakes all around.

20
FISHING PARTY

It was a Sunday with a robin's egg blue sky. The sun was bright with no clouds in sight. We were relishing the idea of a bike ride. Not only because it was a glorious day after several weeks of rain, but due to several months of incredibly delicious dining, we had a guilt complex about our waistlines. The immediate plan was to burn calories.

Like many plans in France, we were waylaid by food.

The perpetrator of our downfall was dear, sweet Marie-France. We had become good friends with her and her husband, Michel – or at least as close friends as people can be when two of the four people speak as though they're still in *école maternelle*, the French equivalent of kindergarten.

Our lack of language skills never daunted Marie-France. She doesn't speak English herself, but her sister does, since she's a French teacher in Great Britain. Marie-France knows what it takes to help the helpless *americains* understand the French language. She speaks clearly and enunciates every word. She chides herself when she speaks too fast. She elbows Michel when he does. Her unfailing efforts rise to providing a word we are stumbling around for. She begins finishing our sentences for us. Sometimes she even finishes our sentences with what we intended to say.

John is filling the bike tires with air when Marie-France calls to announce that Michel would be going fishing. Marie-France is planning to join him and is inviting Annick. While Michel throws lines into the water, the two friends from the Art Association would draw their lines in watercolor. Since it's Sunday, they are planning to spend the day and have a picnic.

Would we like to join them at the lake?

The lake she mentions is just the right distance for a bike ride. We'll meet them there.

"What should we take for our picnic?" John asks.

"No time to get into town. We'll just make sandwiches and throw in some apples and Cokes."

"Sure," he agrees. "That's easy. It'll keep while we bike down there. After all, it's *just* casual, a picnic."

That's how naïve we are.

We load our American-style sandwich picnic into our bike *panniers*. Thus provisioned, we innocently bike down the twisting country road. We ride past the horse farm, through the spot that narrowed to a car's width thanks to a fieldstone house that encroached on the road, and sputter over a short wooden bridge that traverses a stream. We pedal hard up the hill and through the village of Epeigné. On the downhill slope a flat body of water appears ahead. We follow Marie-France's instructions to a narrow path on the west side. It isn't that big a lake and we easily spot their car. We walk the bikes through the screen of the trees.

The usual ant-infested picnic blanket is missing. But nothing else is.

It is a scene straight out of a 19th century Impressionist painting. The painting I have in mind is *Déjeuner sûr Herbe* where nubile young ladies lounge and lunch elegantly on the grass. In this case, the real-life participants are clothed.

In front of us is the most elegant 'simple' picnic ever seen. (The French aptitude for preparing Sunday dinner, even outdoors, still continues to amaze us.) Marie-France and Michel's station wagon had delivered enough equipment to produce a feast of the requisite five courses. And this is just for the three of them, including friend, Annick. We had insisted that we'd pack our own picnic so Marie-France wouldn't have to bother at the last minute.

Marie-France had toted collapsible table and chairs, carefully covered in a flowered tablecloth and set with wine glasses, dishes and silverware. As we enter the picture, she's arranging *hors d'oeuvres* on a platter, while chatting to Annick who is searching through a cooler and comes up with a bottle of wine.

"*Bonjour!*" Michel wanders up from the fishing poles he'd spread out at the edge of the water. We share *les bisous*. Meanwhile, Marie-France chatters non-stop while rummaging through the car for napkins – cloth, of course.

It had taken us longer to arrive than we'd thought. Before five minutes passed Marie-France calls, "*A table.*" Fishing and drawing are put on hold for The Picnic.

With heavy hearts John and I trot back to our bikes where we unload the picnic blanket. We spread it on the ground. Surreptitiously and shamefully we remove the foil-wrapped peanut butter sandwiches and Cokes from our *panniers*. Meanwhile, Marie-France, Michel and Annick are beginning dinner with wine and *hors d'oeuvres*.

John and I are humble hobos watching royalty dine through the glass.

We chat together while the glass divide grows even greater. Two lowly Americans sit on a sad, old plaid blanket with sandwiches, apples and Cokes while   Marie-France, Michel and Annick move from the *hors d'oeuvres* to a first course of ham and asparagus *quiche*. Naturally, they switch from champagne, which worked with the *hors d'oeuvres* to red wine for the next course.

Periodically Marie-France tries to feed us.

"*Non, merci*, we couldn't, we brought our own picnic," we insist.

We watch the main course being served. Cold chicken, fresh garden tomatoes, stuffed eggs, a long baguette.

By the time they reach the cheese course, John and I have hidden the evidence of apple cores. Our French friends offer cheese and insist we try a piece. We each take a delicious slice.

"But you must have wine with the cheese. Please. I brought extra glasses," says Marie-France.

I glance at John who looks at the wine longingly. We give in and let our friends wine and dine us with the leftovers. Then we graciously allow Marie-France to force her homemade cookies on us for dessert.

***

We share coffee (a requisite last course in any decent French dinner), thoughtfully provided by Marie-France via her handy-dandy thermos. Out of nowhere, the sound of the birds becomes a beep beep beep. A cell phone? Out here? That seems a tad high-tech for our retired friends. Besides, the sound isn't coming from us, it is…

Michel runs for his fishing pole.

The traditional scene is forever altered when we inspect Michel's fishing gear more closely. Huck Finn, he isn't. Michel is to fishing what Marie-France is to a French Sunday dinner. He had installed a comfy camp stool near the lake, positioned near the middle of not just one, not just two, but three fishing rods. He had installed a sensing device on each rod that would signal when a fish (or anything else, I supposed) tugged the line. It saved Michel from the arduous task of sitting and watching the rods all day.

Thus, our friend could enjoy his copious French *déjeuner* while still, *en principe*, fishing.

He didn't catch anything. If anyone was a fish out of water, it was the casual Americans. But we learned. Never again will we underestimate the power of the French to maintain traditional standards. Above all else, Sunday dinner would be served.

21
ARE WE DREAMING IN FRENCH YET?

Both my grandmothers had been French, a fact which I hoped meant that buried deep in the recesses of the mind was an inherited gene, connected to the tongue, which would be reconstituted with French wine, enabling me to spontaneously speak French.

This did not happen.

I even had a head start. I'd studied French in high school and college. And I practiced with fervor for the last two years as we were planning our adventure. But what I learned in classes had nothing in common with what I heard in France. Every sentence sounded roughly like "*sahvahalleyseenoopoovohnlefair.*"

John was in worse straits. He had never studied French at all so he started from scratch. Except for one phrase that he had practiced with gusto on previous visits to France: "*Je voudrais du vin, s'il vous plaît.*" He received the requested glass of wine but relied on me for everything else.

Once we decided to live in the French countryside, John diligently applied himself to the study of nouns that have sex. He was sure there was a secret logic to telling the French masculine nouns using the article '*le*' from the feminine nouns using '*la*' and as soon as he discovered that secret, the language would immediately sort itself out. But when he learned that the word *vagin*, for a woman's female part, was masculine he resigned himself to memorizing each article with its noun.

Whenever he became discouraged, I'd remind him of a recent study showing that language learning is superb exercise for the senior-aged brain, keeping it alert and responsive. But alert and responsive, his French wasn't.

Maybe he's just not senior enough.

***

136

French lessons were mandatory. Ordinarily, finding a French teacher in France would not be a problem. People throughout the country speak it quite well, except for us. But our location is outside the major tourist areas and Berlitz doesn't tend to open offices in towns of 3,800 people. We assume that we can find an adult education class. The major problem with this is that adult education classes in France teach English or Spanish or Italian. Except for us, those adults all *know* French.

We consider private lessons. One day at the post office we innocently inquire if anyone knows a French teacher.

The clerks at *La Poste* are two women, each gray-haired and short of stature, nearly hidden behind their service windows. I ask if they know anyone who can tutor us in French.

This is the first error. The slightly portlier Madame, whose name I later learn is Charlotte, has raffish gray-streaked curls and a can-do attitude. She takes our quest as a personal project. With her hair color and can-do attitude it was a distinct possibility that Monsieur Moutrier had a sister.

"Oui, je suis sûr." I'm sure I can find you someone, she claims. But she isn't sure of the phone number. She plans to check the Minitel, which is France's rudimentary text information network, created long before Bill Gates made his first billion.

"Return this afternoon. I will have the phone number for you then."

We do as requested and return at four o'clock. Two people stand in line before us while we wait patiently for Charlotte to be free. She studiously avoids catching our eye. When our turn comes, we don't need stamps. We say hello. We wait. Charlotte's face is downcast. Yes, she found the number for the woman she had considered as our French professor, but the woman is now retired. Charlotte would have to find another teacher.

To avoid any such complications again, she mumbles, "This one must be younger."

As we push out the door, she calls after us, "I may not have the answer today, but I will have it tomorrow!"

As the door swings closed, I looked back. Charlotte's face is wearing worry lines.

The next day we delay until the post office is almost closed, in order to give Charlotte a running start. We don't want to press her. We have the feeling that she doesn't know anyone but she will consider it a personal affront to her skills as a town postmistress if she can't meet the demands of her *clientèle*.

We'd heard that the French often take such tasks seriously and once they promised something, they felt committed to produce. We get the distinct impression that Charlotte feels the pressure.

John and I tell each other that perhaps we are overly concerned. Charlotte had to know that finding a French teacher isn't the end of the world. We have other sources, after all. Maybe we are taking this too seriously ourselves. In any case, she might surprise us by producing a French professor this afternoon.

Charlotte is dejected. She has tried two other people. They weren't right for the task. We would have to return in a few days.

It is the swan song. We'd gone from "come back this afternoon" to "come back tomorrow" to "come back in a few days." It doesn't take someone in Mensa to realize that the pattern is heading toward infinity.

We make other enquiries in the next few days, through American contacts. We avoid *La Poste* where Charlotte works, even going so far as to mail our letters at another village. We can't face showing our faces to Charlotte. It would remind her of the failure to produce a French teacher. Or worse, incite her to further efforts -- and we'd submit ourselves to more fruitless trips to the post office.

We wait two weeks before returning, but we are tired of going kilometers out of our way to visit another post office. We assume that if Charlotte had succeeded in locating a French tutor for us, she'd mention it. If she hadn't, well…

We stand in line after a young woman with an antsy child in tow. Our turn comes. We smile our "*bonjour*" and wait to see what happens.

Charlotte is pleasant. She serves up our stamps. She talks about the weather. She asks about our health. She doesn't mention French teachers. None of us ever speak of it again.

***

Ultimately, we inherit a French teacher from other Americans who live nearby. After ten years in Paris and the Loire Valley, they had definitely graduated. Our new *professeur* is a genteel lady of 73, a widow who is housebound most of the time by severe arthritis. Due to the local grapevine, however, she's gradually accumulated a loyal cadre of Brits, Americans, and Australians who transform her dining room table into a French schoolroom. Madame doesn't limit the lessons to book learning. She includes conversation about local activities and people. She knows more news about who's doing what, where, and how from her dining room chair than anyone walking the streets of town every day.

Best of all, our participation provides a forum for the French sport of discussion. We practice verbs while talking about books and films, the best cathedrals and *châteaux* to visit in France, and French history. *Madame* enjoys sharing personal stories of the war years and the liberation. As a young woman, she joined the hordes of Parisians in the streets to welcome the Allies as they arrived.

"It was *glorieuse* and we were all so happy to be free." She recalls the moment well when she ran toward the line of tanks approaching down the *Champs-Elysées*. Thrilled with the exhilaration of liberation, the young woman waited eagerly for the Americans, proud that she'd studied English and would be able to welcome one of the city's saviors in his own tongue. Rushing to one of the tanks, she began speaking English to the soldier leaning out, only receive a fluent French reply.

In a sea of Americans, *Madame* had found the Canadian from Quebec.

***

Madame urged us to make a pilgrimage to the American Cemetery in Normandy. She recalled her own visit there, years after that day in Paris when she waited for the Allies to arrive. She grew serious and described the neat white rows of crosses and stars of David, each one with a name of an American who'd lost his life in liberating France. We expected her to say that the cemetery was tranquil, impressive, distinguished, sad, or any of a thousand other descriptive adjectives.

To our surprise, she commented gravely that she had felt ashamed. She was ashamed of *herself*. Or rather, ashamed of the young woman who had celebrated on the day the Allies entered Paris.

"I was so happy the day we were liberated…but then I visited the cemetery and I understood that those young men paid the price for my joy."

We made the trip, not expecting much more than an impressive memorial. But the American Cemetery was not a burial ground in which the layer of years has dulled painful memories, where cemetery sleuths feel free to pace about searching "interesting" markers, or comment blithely about the anonymous, long dead names. This experience is fresh, painful and more intense than we'd ever imagined. Perhaps it's a result of being in France, where history is still a rich part of the present. And, yet, we've been in other French cemeteries. This is a different experience altogether, a moving tribute that twists the heart.

As shining and bright as though they were installed yesterday, the pristine white rows of crosses and stars of David fill the manicured lawns with lines of dead. Like a relentless sea, the markers float heavily past the line of vision, overwhelming every other image. Visitors are silent. When they do speak they hush their voices. Steps are measured to a funereal pace.

***

Today, the invasion of Normandy is led by *les tourists*. But the French here have an especially soft spot in their hearts for *les americains*. Several times, when older people met us, they comment that they'd always remember the liberation and bless *les soldats americains*. The blessing somehow carries down the generations to those of us who weren't even born then, but were Americans all the same.

***

Madame is proud of her pupil. Though John has still to achieve the lofty goal of fluency he mutters through most situations. The telephone is the most intimidating situation. Hand signals don't help much. But he eventually advances to making doctor appointments – time, place. Repeat to be sure. Time, place.

Arranging anything technical or mechanical however, still presents a challenge. When the car goes in the shop, we're stopped in our tracks by a double-whammy. Even though I speak more French than my husband, I know nothing mechanical – even in my native language. John knows the mechanical systems, but not the French. Fortunately (or unfortunately, based on the purchase of our ten-year-old *Citroën*) we've become regular visitors to Jacky at the local *garage*.

"Come with me to explain the problem with the car," he says on one of our typical forays to the *Citroën* garage. "You speak French better than I do."

141

I'm pleased to do something worthwhile. OK, to be honest, I'll admit that it's a hoot to show off my French for John. Because he has problems with it, he thinks mine is perfect. Ha!

We trundle off in the ailing vehicle to the repair garage where the entire system of translation breaks down. John takes the lead, in English, and tries explaining the peculiar noise our car engine's making. *Monsieur* Jacky looks puzzled. I jump in to make a rough translation.

John adds some of the possible causes he's considered. He points to gizmos under the hood. I have no idea what he's pointing to.

He includes an erudite analogy between the current problem and his vintage jalopy when he was in college. When he's dug himself in deeply enough, he turns to me in frustration, expecting to be extricated.

He's left me in the dust. I know just how Daniel felt when I breezed ahead in lingo the day I called Rosa's father. Only this time, the lingo is car-speak. My totally un-mechanical frame of reference can't comprehend what my husband explained in *English,* much less in French.

Further French lessons are required, especially after the day I had my comeuppance.

Our trusty *Citroën*'s windshield was pockmarked by a strange combination of age and heat. I visit the insurance agent, who immediately agrees to replace it. No questions asked. All I have to do is visit the repair garage, explain the situation, get the new windshield and submit the bill.

Jacky isn't there that day. I miss his flapping lab coat, which inspires confidence in his diagnostic skills, but the clerk in the service area can handle this situation. Natalie wears jeans and a sweater but despite the lack of a white coat, she's efficient and no-nonsense. She's brown-haired, athletically-built and precise in her motions to the point of appearing stern.

I begin by explaining to Natalie that the insurance will pay to replace a pocked windshield. I bubble on about how "*les boules*" are peppering the glass. I had very efficiently looked up the word for bubbles in the dictionary prior to leaving the house. I feel particularly proud of my ability to communicate in an automotive environment.

Nadia listens politely to my description but when I'm finished she frowns and makes no move to write down the repair order.

"*Les boules*" are in the windshield," I repeat slowly and carefully. Nadia shakes her head as though trying to clear it.

She stands up and comes around her desk. "Perhaps," she says, "we should go look at the car."

I lead the way outside and repeat the explanation, pointing "*les boules*" in the windshield. Nadia's mouth turns up in a smile. She's struggling to stop a laugh but it bubbles up anyway.

Instead of pronouncing the word for "bubbles" in the windshield as "*les bulles*," I'd told her that *les boules*, the heavy metal balls used in the French game of *pétanque,* are in the windshield. Since *boules* are normally rolled along the ground or close to it, my windshield would have been damaged by some maniac *bouliste* with extremely wild pitches.

She explains between giggles. She's still laughing when she pronounces both words.

I admit that I just don't hear a difference." So she pronounces the two words again and, obviously, *she* thinks there's a distinct difference.

I pucker my mouth into what I think is an exact replica of her pronunciation. Nadia shakes her head sadly. "*Non, non. Boules. Bulles. Repetez.*" I try to convey the distinction but fail. Miserably.

"Americans cannot pronounce the 'u,'" she comments with surprising assurance. It implies she is an experienced French professor who has been set down in the middle of a car dealership by error. "We'll work on it."

We practice for fifteen minutes of *"bulles"* and *"boules"* in the parking lot, walking back to the service bay, and in her office. I hate to admit that I still don't hear the difference. Thankfully, I can leave this failure and frustration behind in a few minutes, as soon as the paperwork is completed.

Natalie stops me before I can make my escape.

"One more thing," she admonishes. "Practice the two words...*boules et bulles.*"

"Of course," I agree, knowing full well that I'd never get the knack of those lousy 'u's.

She decided that I wasn't taking the French language seriously enough. Giving me a steely glare, she added the kicker. "Tomorrow, when you come to pick up *la voiture*, you must say them correctly before I can give your car back."

Not wanting to walk for the rest of my stay in France, I spend that evening and the next day muttering *boules, bulles, boules, bulles, bulles, bulles, boules...*

***

Our vocabulary enlarged thanks to diligent practice with *Madame, le professeur*, friends, and a television that initially provided only French channels. As far as the latter is concerned, all went well until we introduced satellite TV to the house, along with NBC, CNN and Eurosport. This one act was responsible for the greatest setback to language skills known to expatriates. Even after two years, three years, four and more, there are always days when French communication goes smoothly. On others...well, the mind goes so smoothly it's numb.

It's said that people achieve the goal of fluency when they begin thinking in French – especially dreaming in it. A friend asked John if this had ever happened to him. He thought a moment, then replied precisely, "Sure, I dream in French ...but I still have no idea what they're saying."

22
WHO US, TOURISTS?

We become snobs about our status in France. We're not (shudder at the thought) tourists. Nope. No way. No how. Hey, John, did you see that beautiful *château*? No, we're not tourists.

After all, we tell ourselves, *we* know the best stalls for fresh mussels. Heck we even call them *moules*. We're natives. Well, about ten times removed.

We are entertaining French friends from Paris for the weekend and they want to see Amboise, just ten minutes north of us. It's a busy Sunday in June and the streets are packed with gawkers. Amboise is a pretty town, though some of its charm is disguised behind its hordes of tourists. The sidewalk tables are filled with them, trying to translate the menus or practicing their high school French. The shops sell more postcards and replicas of French landmarks than anything else. Americans and Brits that we pass are snapping photos of the clock tower, the pastry windows, and the sausages hanging in the *charcuterie*.

The four of us stroll in the warm sun, Ann-Marie and I out front, John and Daniel trailing behind. John stops in an *épicerie* for a bottle of water and Daniel follows him while Anne-Marie and I chat on the street just outside the door.

By this stage John's French had progressed past requesting wine. He could order water. But his accent is thicker than a French wall. He hems and haws. He halts. During this, Daniel is standing directly behind him, wearing the Atlanta Braves cap we'd given him the year before.

The store clerk waiting on John is a portly man with a receding hairline. He says something to John, who waits for the bottle of water but has no idea what the man said.

Daniel steps forward.

Ann-Marie and I hear the normally placid Daniel from the street and run inside to see what the commotion's all about.

"You should be ashamed of yourself for being rude," he blasts at his fellow countryman.

The clerk turns red. How was he to know that the man of the Atlanta baseball cap, whose buddy is this American tourist, could actually understand his snide comment? The crowded store comes to a halt as they enjoy Daniel's lesson in *politesse*.

The impatient French clerk would be more careful in the future.

***

Two years later we don't even remember which store it was. And Sunday in Amboise is the best replacement for the Sunday mornings in Atlanta when we'd enjoy a lazy morning brunch out.

In France it's one of the first things we missed, this ability to go out for breakfast -- especially on gray days when the foot-thick Sunday paper would keep us content over extra cups of coffee for hours.

One time the winter doldrums had already set in for a week of cold wet and gray days. On Sunday, we wake early and discover *l'été indienne* has arrived. This bright Indian summer day translates into the sudden urge to be outside at the Amboise Sunday market.

Even better, it's late in the year, off-season for the tourist hordes. We would miss the array of bikes with baskets, white tennis shoes, and happy English, Americans, Dutch, and Germans snapping each other's pictures outside the cafés. We would be able to select the produce at the huge outdoor Amboise market without the crowds.

See it we did, wandering the several blocks of bounteous fresh foods and mounds of mums in purple, gold and yellow. We glory in finding things that weren't evident in our smaller town's market like fresh guava and black mushrooms. The latter are midnight in color and slimy and shaped like trumpets. Thus, their name, *Trompettes de*

146

Mort– the trumpets of death. When John suggests mushroom soup, I suggest not.

The variety is overwhelming. We want to buy it all and vow to return more often – and to resist shopping next Saturday so the refrigerator would be empty next Sunday.

When our feet give out we stroll until we find a café with tables in the sun. The one we choose happens to be at the foot of the ramp leading to the *Château d'Amboise*. The tables face the bell tower with its clock and turret and the cobbled pedestrian street -- a tourist spot if we ever saw one. But if there are tourists here they appear to be French ones. Even the couple next to us, whom we suspect of being German when we see her ordering beer at ten o'clock in the morning, is soon heard speaking French.

We order coffee and John sit and sketches. I watch the human and canine parade. The street is busy. The sun has drawn out the French for Sunday morning market and, like us, many of them have decided it's much too nice a day to return home in a hurry. *"On doit profiter."* They say often. One must profit from the opportunity to enjoy.

A young chef's assistant trots past in his white jacket, carrying a basket. A last minute errand before the market stands shut for the day?

Young couples wander past with babies in strollers. I watch two such couples together. The man drops his cigarette stub on the ground and steps on it. His wife nudges him. He stoops down and picks it up to deposit it in the trash bin.

Today is a good day for the dogs' day out. One arrived with its people, which started a discussion with the two women next to them on the breed and the cuteness.

The beer-drinking woman and man next to us are, like us, dog-less and kid-less and simply enjoying the sun. We've been here enjoying the sun for well over an hour. Eventually this lessens the typical French reserve. We smile at them.

The man leans over his wife to ask me, "Do you have a knife?"

"A knife?" Have we discovered a only madman in this peaceful scene? I start to look for the waiter to pay quickly.

"*Oui*," the man answers.

His wife fumbles in the basket at her feet and brings out a plastic bag filled with sausages. John sees them and grabs his pocket knife.

"We'll share," said the French man. He saws off a large portion and hands it to John, then slices one for me. His wife provides the commentary on where we can find the sausage and the fact that they found the large oval delicacies at just ten *saucissons* for a hundred francs.

They're from Tours, the large city to the west. Like us, they were attracted to Amboise today by the unseasonably warm weather and the massive market. Other than "profiting from the good times" one must "change ideas" occasionally. Changing ideas is related to the philosophy of pleasure. One must get out and relax, try something new. Visiting another town market suffices.

The woman leans over and peeks at John's drawing of the clock tower. "*Pas mal*" she says. It's the greatest French compliment. "Not bad." Which means really good.

Oui, we respond, again raising our faces to the sun. "*Pas mal. Pas mal*" at all.

23
LIKE WATCHING PAINT DRY

The game of *pétanque* is not covered by ABC, NBC, CNN or Eurosport. It's never made it to the Olympics. It could even be argued that the majority of the world's population outside of France, have no earthly idea that *pétanque* even *is* a sport.

For its adherents, however, *pétanque* rises to the level of a religious experience. Higher if one considers that the truly converted *pétanque* player would miss Sunday services, but would never dream of missing his regular *pétanque* match.

To be fair, a few people recognize the game by another name since it's also called *boules* in some areas of France. The game is roughly similar to the Italian game of *bocce*.

It's a simple game. Players throw a hefty steel ball, the *boule*, which is the size of a tennis ball, towards a small wood ball, called a *cochonnet,* which could be crushed to splinters if one of the heavy metal fellows ever landed square on it. This is extremely unlikely and the game's creators must have understood the impossibility since the word *cochonnet,* or piglet, is extremely close to the verb *cochonner*, which means to bungle.

The object of the game is simply to see who gets closer. In this way, *pétanque* is very much like horseshoes except that horseshoes stay put once they land. In *pétanque*, the balls thud dully onto hardpacked earth and roll or bounce – as much as a heavy metal object can bounce – into other metal balls. Part of the joy is trying to knock another player's ball out of position. In this respect, *pétanque* is the heavy-metal version of croquet.

The players, called *boulistes*, are divided into 'placers' – the ones who are good at getting the team's ball into good position – and *tireurs* or 'bombers.' The latter are the Rambos of *pétanque*. They play after the opposing team has already thrown and placed one or more *boules* closest to the cochonnet. Their mission is to blast the other team into oblivion.

Sound exciting? It might be if any of the players moved faster than French snails. However, the unwritten rules of *pétanque* require that the game be played with a careful deliberation that would put a nuclear engineer or astronaut to shame.

In *pétanque* most energy is expended in arguing about who's closest to the *cochonnet*. Special retracting metal rods and rulers exist in order to measure which *boule* is that silly little millimeter farther away. It could be mentioned that the other national sport of France is *le foot,* which is at the opposite end of the activity spectrum.

Football players move.

Mostly, *pétanque* enables the Frenchman to give his love of discussion full play. Before a ball is thrown, the team discusses their strategy, decides who will act as placer and who as bomber, and determines the best wine to choose as their reward should they win. More serious discussion takes place among all players after the balls are thrown. Each person adds his opinion of its merits: Is it closer or farther? Did it bounce higher or skid longer or kick another ball out of place properly? How did the ball curve? The game thus played becomes an exercise in talk.

Nothing comes to blows. No matter how vehement the discussion becomes, no muscle is activated other than the mouth.

The mouth is activated again when all this frenetic activity recesses for refreshments. Then the wine bottle appears. (In southern France, cultural distinctions call for this to be *pastis*, a powerful licorice flavored drink) Nothing looks much different to a *pétanque* audience since the players move at the same speed drinking as they do playing. They continue to talk, though the subject is now a rehash of the previous plays, interspersed by comparing local wines.

Now, how do I know all these intimate details on the game of *pétanque*. I haven't the patience to play the game, much less to watch it. My husband does both. Every week. Like clockwork. *Pétanque* is popular in France with those who have the time it takes to spend discussing each move, which is in large part retirees, a category in which John happily counts himself. He loves the game. He loves sitting on park benches watching the players. He loves the way the players precisely measure the distances between balls with the official tape, calling out who's closer to the *cochonnet* and announcing who throws next. Basically John loves all this because he has a patience that I lack. On one of the rare occasions where I've gone near the field I noticed that it took a half hour just for the players to gather and shake hands.

I do the laundry and watch it spin.

***

John has yet to wear his navy beret playing *pétanque* but that doesn't prevent him from becoming a card-carrying *bouliste,* a member of the local *pétanque* group. This permits him to enter the local *tournois*, or *pétanque* tournaments.

Any serious *bouliste* wouldn't miss one. Thus, my husband's first tournament will be an exciting event – well, as a comparative term. To John's great disappointment, he doesn't make the final cut but he does learn the lay of the *terre,* so to speak. By the second tournament he has the ground rules down pat and is going for the gold. He even visits the town park while the other *boulistes* are busy lunching for two-and-a-half hours to get some practice in on the sly. He practices underhand rolls, flipping his wrist jauntily, to create his version of a *boule* bombing run. The tournament date is fast approaching. Would he be the American fool in last place? Can he at least make a strong showing?

The pressure mounts. His practice time increases.

The great day dawns and John gathers his three *boules,* his American baseball cap, and sunglasses an hour before the tournament.

"Where are you going so early?" "Gotta warm up my stroke," says the pro.

He hops on his bike and sets off for the empty park. In wifely devotion, I wait until the time of the tournament. By the time I arrive the contestants are mostly standing in hand-shaking groups, warming up their mouths for the discussion to follow. Off to one side, several men set out supplies of local red wine for the breaks. The local ladies' group arranges cookies to go with it.

At three o'clock, the games begin. It is a team sport but each player will earn points for matches won, while playing with different partners. They will switch partners five times, presumably to even out the playing field. The winner will be the player with the most points after five matches.

As his first partner John draws the best player in the group, a patriarchal figure of a man called 'Grand Jean.' Their team is off and rolling. As John later explains in his recap, "I had to play well. I didn't want to look terrible in comparison."

They win that match.

The second match of the day John is partnered with his best friend on the team – the man who recruited John originally, Pierre. Pierre is one of the better local players.

They win their match. When I catch up to John for that after-game interview, he notes, "I just couldn't let Pierre down. After all, he'd lose points if we lost."

The third and fourth matches are with weaker partners and John loses one of them. But other opponents are having a bad day and fold early. That makes three matches out of four that John has won, one of them, the first, by a wide margin, giving him a position near the front of the pack.

Meanwhile, Grand Jean and Pierre have played on teams against each other. Grand Jean won, so Pierre lost a few points. On another of his matches, Grand Jean lost by a hair.

The scoring is getting complicated and as the play winds down at the end of the afternoon John loses count of the individual points. He knows he's in the top group. So are Grand Jean and Pierre but it occurs to John that he actually stands a good chance of winning.

It is possible that he, the American, would show up the great Grand Jean who has played this national sport of *pétanque* all his 67 years. Or, John would take the prize from his friend Pierre.

He doesn't want to win.

The fifth match is on. John's partner is a nice older man who is a good 'bomber' to John's placement skills. To hear John tell it, the tension was worse than a million-dollar business presentation. "What was I to do? I couldn't throw the match because that would be throwing it for my partner's points as well. I had to find that final reserve of strength."

He did.

Fearing that this last win has put him into the winner's circle John tries to hide inconspicuously at the back of the crowd. The officials count the points. They count them again. John breathes a sigh of relief. Grand Jean has won first prize. John ties for second – with Pierre.

Each winner wins a trophy and gets to choose from the bottles of liquor – what else? John chooses last.

The trophy's in his office. The whiskey's gathering dust in our liquor cabinet. His friendships on the *pétanque* court remain intact.

24
TROGLODYTE TALES

Troglodyte. The word sounds straight from the Jurassic era, with images of dinosaurs, murky bogs plus an ogre or two just waiting to pop out from deep dark caves. That's not too far from the truth. Age-wise, anyway. The *troglodyte* caves of France's Loire Valley have pocked this area for centuries. At first the natural limestone caves made convenient homes for the earliest residents. Then shepherds who couldn't make it home used them as shelter. Later, masons mined the stone, lengthening the caves into massive galleries that sometimes run for miles beneath the earth. The resulting stone blocks bear a strong resemblance to a giant's white Lego blocks. They serve as the thick walls of the numerous *châteaux*.

Our medieval *donjon* in town was built of the local *tuffeau* stone. It's crumbling and, in some spots, blackened with age and battle. A fair amount of the *le donjon* was destroyed during World War II. But the square tower still lords it over Montrichard and the Cher river valley. Despite its jagged, wounded walls it's an impressive sight, especially at night when the town spotlights the tower in an ocher glow as it stands as a sentinel over the city at its feet.

***

For several months we had seen advertisements for a *tuffeau* cave home that is open to visitors in the nearby town of Bourré. One brisk October morning we decide to see for ourselves what one of these residences is like. We leave our car where indicated on the shoulder of the road from town and follow the signs. They lead up a narrow private road that curves steeply toward the cliff. There are countless openings, some with shutters at the so-called windows, others are closed with wooden doors.

The sign says that the cave tour is available but when we arrive at the courtyard it's empty. Not a soul is in view and, it being out of season, we wonder if we're mistaken. Then we see a sign. "For tour, ring the bell."

In this environment we expect to see someone closer to the cave era -- perhaps a grizzled, gray-haired woman or man. Instead, a young man of about thirty (thick black hair, not a gray one in sight) answers the summons. Would we like a tour? he asks. We'd get to see the cave house, the tunnels, and, he adds proudly, his silk farm. That we can't miss.

He speaks some English and is happy to practice on us during our private tour.

Looking up at the cliff, dark holes appear that are fitted with doors and windows. I'd heard people lived in cave houses, but I compare it to camping out. Perhaps one did "live" there as a vacation experience but not full time. This did not fully explain the satellite dishes that pop up at odd angles on the cliffs.

The weather is crisp. John and I are already shivering in anticipation – literally – as we imagine the cold, damp caves. The young man leads us toward a thick wooded door, formally set into a lintel of carved stone. On both sides of it is solid stone. We are about to enter the darkened recesses of *tuffeau* tunnels. We zip up our windbreakers to prepare and hope our eyes will adjust quickly to the darkness. Where are the flashlights, the lamps? The young man opens the door and asks us to follow him. We enter the black hole.

Except, the space is luminous. It creates a new dimension, like a foray into a Martian laboratory. The walls are luminously white as though someone has hidden recessed lighting in the crevices. It is simply the white *tuffeau* reflecting every ray of sun that can enter.

"*Le salon*," the young man explains as we pass into a high vaulted chamber with fireplace. That explains the chimneys we'd seen sticking out of the cliffs. We pass through a shadowed hall, and enter a small room with a window built into the stone. "This was the bedroom my brother and I shared," says the young man. The space is pristine white, about ten by twelve feet, barely furnished now with a chest of drawers and single bed but nothing else.

"We've moved to the house," he explains and points down and out the window to a simple three walled rectangle with a roof that extrudes from the cliff, which made up the fourth side. High on one wall is a satellite dish.

Another bedroom is also empty of furnishings. Apparently they'd been needed in the newer house next door. We enter a sculptural room that would have made a terrific modern art gallery. The walls are the sculptures. Roughly curving arches appear to have been shaped by nature. Undulating shapes poke from the walls. They could have been considered figural in form but only if the sculptor had been Van Gogh translating his frantic brush strokes into three dimensions.

We mount three stone steps and follow a gently ascending ramp to another level. Niches in the narrow passage hold glass containers filled with squiggly creatures. We've reached the famous silk worms. A small room at the end of the passage displays the stages in a silk worm's life, done in hand lettering. The young man spends more time explaining his hobby than he had explaining the *tuffeau* house itself. Unfortunately, by now he has reverted to French, which is easier for him. Considering his English, it might even have been easier for us too. Not perfect, but at least we had an excuse for not understanding what he said. Especially the technical explanations of the silkworms' mating process.

We spend most of his discourse checking out the view from the window. It's like being an eagle perched in a cozy nest high on the cliffs. The Cher river winds one-dimensionally in gray-blue. The patchwork of fields ranges from vivid yellow colza to blue-green vineyards to softer hues of pasture land.

The *tuffeau* home is a nicer place to visit than I had thought. I still wouldn't want to live there.

***

It was time to visit another set of tuffeau caves, but this time we thirsted after the Caves Monmousseau. No one extols living in these unless it's a wino who wants to be lost in paradise. These caves are reserved for wine storage. A lot of wine storage. Over the decades a massive mining operation hollowed out the tunnels under the cliffs to a distance of 15 kilometers, about 12 miles. Not all of it is straight. Extensions head off at all angles. And, let's face it, one tuffeau tunnel looks pretty much like another tuffeau tunnel.

During our tour, the sprightly guide tells our group of fifteen, "Please, do not wander away to explore. We don't find the skeletons until years later."

I assumed he was joking.

Actually, the rumors about town hold that during the Occupation, German troops had used the deep underground caverns at Monmousseau to store ammunition and other supplies. The deep caves, many with tunnels wider than a two-lane highway, provided hiding spots and protection from attack without the need to dig in. According to locals, German lorries are still rusting away back in the farthest tunnels. And, some German soldiers didn't listen to *their* guide. They wandered off, without a proper map, and were never seen again. Their skeletons, they say, have never been found.

When the woman says, "Don't wander off" we don't. Our skeletons plan to make it back in order to sample the wine Monmousseau pours at the end of the tour. (If you go, get in at the end of the line and look like a serious *connoisseur*. You can make it through cocktail hour this way.)

***

After drinks, our dinner was fit for a caveman. A mile down the road from Monmousseau is the *Deux Caves*. It's a simple grill-style restaurant that made the two caves for which it's named into a dining hall. You don't have to be a spelunker to dine. From the tables,

157

you can see through the arched doorway to the outdoor patio.(It soothes any tendency toward claustrophobia.) Most visitors like the novelty of dining inside the cliff.

The dining room walls are rough, as stone should be. Every six feet or so, someone had carved out a niche and placed a small lamp inside. Very charming, despite the electric wiring that threaded from one to the other. (You don't exactly run wiring through stone.) The tables are simple wood, decked out in blue and white checked tablecloths, with heavy white crockery.

Looking at tables filled with well-fed diners calls to mind those German skeletons. No, we wouldn't starve to death in this cave. Dining underground, I presume, calls for energy and the warmth of solid filling fare. This grill, like the others is known for its good home cooking and plenty of it. Sure, it's not the gourmet cuisine with elegant sauces for which French chefs are famous. This is down-to-earth – literally -- cooking.

Thick slabs of meat pate arrive in a huge white crock. It's left on the table to be served family style. It comes in handy for anyone who wants to make a true pig of himself. (The French never seem to do this. Only we Americans are tempted to partake of a second, third, or fourth helping.)

One evening we take a visiting American friend here. As soon as the hostess seats us I remember that Lynne is a vegetarian. We look over the menu. Beef, lamb, pate. Of course, it's a grill. I apologize profusely and suggest that we could leave. Lynne notes there are French fries and salad and grilled mushrooms, no problem.

Meanwhile, she's eying that big crock of *paté*. She mutters something about being on vacation. And digs in.

Apparently her philosophy is once a sinner, always a sinner. Lynne follows the *paté* with lamb grilled with rosemary. She doesn't even have the grace to look guilty as she polishes it off. It's served with a sizzling platter of potatoes to share. Then the cheese course, of

158

course. And desert for anybody who still has the will to eat an apple tart or ice cream. Then coffee.

We waddle outside in the fresh night air, the sizzling smell of grilling lamb behind us. The waist on my jeans feels far too snug. I think of the skeletons in their cave. Nope, we definitely don't have that problem.

25
BOOKED AGAIN: *La Chambre d'Amis*

Nothing equals the attraction of friends living in France. Not even the Eiffel Tower since the Eiffel Tower won't feed you *croissants*, drive you to a dozen different *châteaux,* and insulate you from the difficulties of dealing with another language.

When we first moved to France, we threw caution to the winds and freely issued invitations to family, friends, co-workers, the dentist who loves France, his dental hygienist who was standing behind him ready to attack our tartar -- anyone, in fact, for whom we felt the slightest good will.

"If you're ever in France, be sure to come see us." The open door policy was big enough to drive a 747 through.

The enthusiasm for covering 360 degrees with invitations was easy to rationalize. After all, we felt incredible fortunate to be living this wonderful life and we did want to share it. Besides, with an ocean separating us from these hundreds of potential guests, how many people could actually take us up on it?

We found out.

We had more company across the ocean in the first six months than we had when living in Atlanta for six years. Most of our visitors said something to the effect of, "We wanted to visit while you were still here." The implication, not thinly veiled, was that we'd soon turn tail and run back to the states. They all intended to visit before we did.

It wasn't necessary to issue formal invitations. Our nearest and dearest hundred friends and acquaintances would find us, even if we changed our address, our name, and went undercover with the protected witness program.

That is not to say we didn't enjoy each and every visitor. We're thrilled to have them join us for two reasons:

First, we can enjoy seeing them here instead of us going there. That beats us taking the nine-hour plane trip away from our daily fresh-baked baguette.

Second, we get a real kick out of seeing the Loire Valley through the fresh eyes of American visitors who, if they do their tourist duties properly, will admire the stone carving on the various *châteaux*, the deep green of a peaceful river valley, the food markets packed with fresh foods without plastic wrappings, and wine tastings that would make even Scrooge effusive with joy.

To date, no one has surpassed the enthusiasm of our very first visitors. Lynne, the vegetarian, called two weeks before our furniture was due to arrive.

"You'll never guess," she said.

She was right, I wouldn't.

"There's this great deal, air fare to Paris for $250."

"Sounds wonderful."

"It's a weekend."

"You're coming from Atlanta to Paris for a weekend!"

"Sure, why not. Oh, and I've got a friend who'll come with me. You'll like her."

"Love to see you…err both…but I thought those deals were hard to come by."

"Nah, found it on Travelocity. It's one of those last-minute things"

The sinking feeling began in my throat and traveled to my sour stomach.

"Ummm, Lynne, *when* is this?"

"Next weekend."

"Ahhh, Lynne… well, that is, ummm, that's when our furniture's arriving. I mean, it doesn't get here until Thursday. And you arrive…?"

"Friday. But don't worry, we won't be there 'til afternoon."

"The house will be torn up."

"We don't mind."

"Ummmm, Lynne, what about beds, I don't know if they'll be set up."

"No problem, we'll sleep on the floor."

"Ummmm, Lynne. Ummmm, well, gee, that sounds just, ummm, great."

The welcome mat would have been out, if we could have found it in the packing crates. Our first guests arrived the day after the very same move that required a marathon run up and down four levels with the circus act of installing two mammoths into the second floor.

I was still running the next day, on nervous energy, wanting our first guests to see the house as I imagined it could be. Instead, they'd be crunched between packing crates, sleeping on one if we couldn't get the beds together in time.

I thought of Martha Stewart and shuddered.

We set the alarm the morning after moving day (and night) and drag ourselves up. We had promised to pick Lynne and her friend up at the TGV station in St. Pierre des Corps, where the fast train from Paris would deposit them. Lynne's "afternoon" arrival was one p.m. but we'd have to leave a little after noon to make the 45-minute trip and find parking, always a difficult problem near the station.

In the daze of exhaustion we attack the cartons in the living room, pulling pots and pans and dishes from the cartons, washing and dusting these articles that had sat in storage for six months, then shipped across the ocean. The task is complicated by the fact that every square inch, except for a narrow path, is covered with something that has to be moved again before we can get at another box. Each time we empty a box, we flatten it to give ourselves more space in the living room. The stomping down on the carton unleashes feelings of accomplishment. Until we count. Three empty boxes. By nine-thirty it becomes apparent that this method will never clear a path to the guest room. The neat approach gives way to piling scads of newspaper wrappings in a corner as we dump cups and plates and pans into cupboards and slam the doors behind them. No one would look in there anyway. They couldn't even *see* the doors for the mess.

It's getting close to eleven. We have to leave by noon to make it to the train station in time. The atmosphere combines the panic of the stock market on Black Tuesday and Times Central Station during rush hour.

John is assigned to the guest room where he starts putting together the bed frames. I search through boxes labeled linens to find the bedding that fit. I paw through more linens than I remember owning, and pull out more sheets that are queen size than the singles required.

At 11:20 Lynne calls from Paris to announce they'd missed the first train to Tours. John and I look at each other and breathe a sigh of relief. We've gained two extra hours. He manages to get the beds together and I make the beds. They aren't Martha's neat hospital corners, but they are sleep-able. We drag boxes we don't have time to unpack into the adjacent hall. Our first guests will have to stumble around the boxes to reach the bathroom, but at least they can move around in the guest room itself.

We make it to the train station five minutes late but that doesn't faze Lynne and Jodie. The living room is stacked with boxes that we'd shoved into one corner but it is an improvement over the total chaos that had reigned in the previous hours. Lynne and Jodie love the house anyway.

***

Our guests had been on the plane all night from Atlanta. Naturally, we thought, they'd rest up. Which meant we could. We'd have dinner out. That we could manage.

"So, I imagine you're a little tired," I hint. Feel a little jet-lagged?" Even to myself, I sound like a commercial.

"Nah, not bad," says Lynne.

"I'm sure you must be tired. The beds are together. I'll show you the guest room and you can rest up."

"Oh, we don't want to waste a minute. We only have the weekend, you know."

"You're here 'til Monday, then?" I ask, calculating when I'd be able to get my home in shape. And sleep.

***

I did sleep. If sleepwalking counts. Our first visitors earn the award of most enthusiastic – and most energetic. They are thrilled to see France and exude the energy of teenagers rather than forty-somethings. They use exclamation points at every *château*, every beret-clad citizen, every food item that comes within taste or shop window. We hear none of the "Yuck, I couldn't eat *that*," of some guests who notice a market stall selling snails or plump, dead rabbits.

There is method in their charm. Lynne and Jodie easily encourage us to leave the unpacking and traipse all over with them. They don't even complain when Saturday arrives cold and damp. We go into Blois to see the *château* and a cartoon conference John had read about. Cartoon books, even for adults, are popular in France. There are detective cartoons, romantic cartoons, and double x-rated cartoons.

The ladies and I tour the chateau while John ogles primary colors in square blocks at the conference. Later, when the rain begins, we have the perfect excuse to stop for rich, dark *café* and lemony tarts at my favorite pastry shop on rue du Commerce.

The coffee keeps John and I on our feet. Barely. Exhausted, soaked with rain from a final downpour, and ready for home, the four of us scurry back to the car. It's dusk and the lights come on in the parking lot as we approach. But the lights don't come on in the car when John turns the key. Probably because the lights had already been on for the entire day we'd spent in Blois.

The battery is, in a word, *morte.*

I glare at John, the driver, the culpable, the husband. I want to get home, go to bed, to sleep, perchance to dream. But we can't go anywhere.

Did our visitors utter even one word of discouragement? No. They sum up the situation quickly. To save our marriage and keep the home intact in which they plan to spend that evening, they go to work.

Lynne opens the rear door and stands outside the car.

"I'll take care of this," she announces.

"What are you going to do?" I ask.

Lynne doesn't speak French. She doesn't know anyone except us, the fellow strandees, in the country. She doesn't have to.

Lynne boldly heads a few yards toward the road and puts on the flirtiest expression she can muster. She flags down the first driver she sees. It's a young man and his friend who are charmed out of their jumper cables.

As I said, some guests are real gems.

***

Our next set of guests waited to make reservations until we unpacked. Marsha had a new beau.

"It's serious," my long-single friend says. "Can I bring him with me?

"Of course," I reply. "We'd love to meet him."

That was a month before they arrived. By the time they walk in the house they are having a running argument and Marsha is so busy contending with her romantic life that the Loire takes a backseat.

The boyfriend is pleasant but if we thought he wanted to see France, we had another think coming. For his ten-day visit to France he has carted his entire short wave set with him. He brought the frequencies of various French people he had "met" via short wave in the states.

One morning he leaves early to install the short wave antenna in a propitious location. He arrives back at our Loire Valley house and proudly announces that he had reached a Frenchman on short wave.

The next morning he convinces Marsha to go with him. She may have envisioned a wonderful day spent exploring the wonders of France. Perhaps that would have revived the relationship.

But by mid-afternoon she reports back that boyfriend had spent half the time climbing a tree in an attempt to raise the antenna higher for better reception.

He, on the other hand, is thrilled to announce that he'd reached several more French people from this jury-rigged set-up arranged in the rental car.

We wonder why he didn't just go down the street and talk to them.

***

When he isn't shortwaving, boyfriend is jogging. We provide a key to the wrought iron gate out front. It locks automatically and I don't want him to be locked out. Nor do I want to jump up to let guests in every time they go out. We do that for Folly, but heck, that's our sweet little dog. These guests are human. Not to mention younger and vastly more energetic than we are.

Boyfriend could remember dozens of short wave frequencies, but he couldn't remember to take the key to the front gate. Whenever he goes out, he rings the bell to get in until I feel like Pavlov's dog. After several times of my reminding him, apparently even *he* decides he can't ring the bell again. He left to go jogging at 6:30 a.m. and on the way back realizes he's locked out but decides that his athletic prowess would solve the problem. He jogs around the block and tries climbing the hill below our backyard. He slips and slides and in general makes a spectacle that the people in the nursing home behind us enjoy as their morning entertainment.

When this effort doesn't succeed in his reaching the heights of our house, he returns to study the front gate more seriously. He studies the foot-high pointed spears above it and imagines himself jumping up there and trying to crawl over them in his little running shorts.

Deciding not to risk the family jewels, he rings the bell. Again.

26
PEARLS OF CULTURE

We planned a trip to discover a new area of France. After all, that's why we were living in the Loire. Folly would stay with the love of his life, Nadia. But our other faithful companion, the Citroën, would get us where we wanted to go. Jacky at the garage would see that it did.

We'd never been to the Alps so we headed toward Chamonix and the famous Mont Blanc. We want to see the real thing, not just a namesake pen.

We travel along a French *Route Nationale*. These roads are good and in some stretches they can be free-flowing but often they go through towns which slows things down. They often parallel the fast *autoroutes*, but they don't charge tolls and you get to see the scenery instead of fearless French *Grand Prix* drivers. Nevertheless we are making good time. We have just determined that we'd be eating lunch within the hour at our destination when the traffic slows. The speedometer edges lower and lower. Soon we are creeping at an *escargot*'s pace.

"An accident?" we guess. "Road work?" Cars are jammed together far beyond the corner ahead. We can't tell what is happening or how long the line of stopped cars is. Our car crawls forward a few more yards. A car length. Another car length. Fifteen minutes go by. We draw closer to flashing lights and see several gendarmes managing traffic in the road up ahead. We gawk. It is safe at our speed, which is next to nothing. We watch for crushed fenders, ambulances, fire trucks, construction crews. Nothing.

Still, there are all those lights and gendarmes on both sides of the road. We are close enough now to see the gendarmes stopping traffic. Cars creep up to them from both directions.

"A traffic control check?" Are they searching for an escaped international drug lord?

Our turn comes and the *Citroën* inches up to a fine figure of a young gendarme. He gestures for John to roll down the window. We are curious. Ok, so we are also a tad nervous. Why is he stopping us? I review mentally. Yes, we have a current *vignette* showing we've paid our taxes. We have our insurance certificate. Jacky checked out the car before we'd left. We have on our seatbelts.

The gendarme thrusts a clipboard at John. He begins explaining something. John doesn't understand. I had been so busy reviewing our car's legal condition I hadn't listened. The gendarme pushes the clipboard farther into the car so it rests on the steering wheel in front of John who stares at it like a snake.

"Could you repeat that?" I ask.

"Would you please sign our petition?" the gendarme requests with a smile.

"A petition? What kind of petition?"

"The Ministry of Education is closing the school in town," he explains. "We are collecting the signatures to keep the school open."

The gendarmes, with their power to corral the public, are applying it to education.

"But we don't live in the area." My accent makes that clear enough. We don't live in this town. We don't live in this *departement*. We don't live in this region of France. We aren't even French. Obviously, we can't sign his petition.

"*Bien sûr*," he replies. "It does not matter. Anyone can sign." He points to the line. Implacably.

"If you say so…" With a flourish we add our names to the next two lines on the thick sheaf of papers on the clipboard.

He waves the clipboard in a goodbye salute and we breeze on our way. We pass cars lined up in the opposite direction for half a kilometer. We wonder what all these people in the cars snaking toward the gendarmes from both directions will say when they find out why they are being hijacked.

How much ya wanna bet that school stayed open?

***

Home from that trip, we need to replenish the refrigerator so we stop at the grocery store. As we are checking out, Kahlil Gibran is sitting next to the checkout counter. Well, his book is, anyway. *Le Prophète* in French stares up at me, in a rack where most Americans see *TV Guide*, *People*, and the *National Enquirer*. All the material that is suitable for "inquiring minds" that want to know who did what to whom, whether in la-la land or the soaps.

The French save the cheesy stuff for the dairy section. In France, philosophy makes it into the cart with the *chèvre*.

Philosophy is not a dirty word in France. When I buy the first book in the Harry Potter series in an English bookstore at Tours, the title seems different. Is it another book in the same series? But, no, this is listed as the first book. But the title was "Harry Potter and the Philosopher's Stone." Fair enough. Except, when I see the book later in the United States the title is *Harry Potter and the Sorcerer's Stone*. Why the title change when J.K. Rowling wrote the original in English? Later I learned that an editor assumed that, unlike little Europeans, American children could not be expected to know the word 'philosophy.' The title was switched to Sorcerer's as in *The Sorcerer's Apprentice*.

A Mickey Mouse cartoon. Who says Americans have no culture?

***

Being a paragon of culture is a heavy burden. The French take on the task with aplomb, bearing the stress of a high intellectual standard. They proudly claim the Louvre, the Musée d'Orsay, and

170

regular student protests for more professors and better learning conditions.

Even the general population follows its educational progress rigorously. In June, our French television programming includes a curious scroll at the bottom of the screen. It consists of a *mélange* of numbers and many of them have percentage marks behind them. Normally in the states such scrolls are reserved for election results, sports scores, and emergency weather warnings. With numbers like 4,800 that seems like a pretty high wind.

We are mesmerized by the numbers. Like intrepid spies we try breaking the code as numbers scrolled below game shows, movies, and news. We notice just one constant, the initials BAC. Our powers of observation and knowledge of the culture don't supply the answer. Finally, I asked Annick. "The BAC scores," she said. "Baccalaureate." The results from the student test would determine the students' future and the state of education in France.

Heck, if Kahlil Gibran makes it to the checkout, why not BAC scores on the TV.

27
THE MADONNA SEES ALL

Across the street from our house is a tall *tuffeau* cliff. A polychrome wood statue of the Virgin Mary stands at the second-story level, in an arch hewn from the stone. She faces directly toward our house, a protector of sorts, standing guard night and day.

Below the statue are caves that belong to a more modern *bourgeoise* house (a relative term since it's only a century old). The caves across from us aren't as massive as the tunnels in town or at Monmousseau. Nevertheless, before Renault and Citroën arrived in France, the central cave came in handy as a place to store the horse-pulled carriage. Monsieur, who rents an apartment in the subdivided house, explained one day that the small square stone that's positioned precisely in the center of the largest cave entrance had a purpose. It permitted the carriage driver to back up the horse, aligning the carriage wheels over the block so as to enter the cave without scraping the carriage along the side.

It's the statue, however, that draws my attention. I'm not particularly religious, but the lady above is a lovely piece of roughhewn art from yesteryear. The colors are faded now but they have a rich patina; someone had lovingly painted it originally. The statue is old and presumably it managed to outlast the Nazis so that's something. The blue-gowned figure is a comfort, somehow, as she benignly watches over us. Too soon, the time came when comfort was needed.

***

Our doctor announced that John's heart was beating erratically. With my inexact understanding of cardiac technicalities, his heart rhythm needed 'conversion.' The term sounded like a Bible thumping religious experience but it translated to meaning that his heart had to be shifted from a thumpity thump squoosh thump to a thump thump thump thump.

An electric cardioversion would shock him into rhythm.

***

The shock procedure did not, apparently, work like a solution for hiccups. I couldn't simply put a werewolf head on, sneak up on John and say boo. He'd need a strong jolt of electricity to do the job.

John's stateside cardiologist had already done the procedure on him once before, but his heart reverted to its bad habits. So here we are in France, with John's heart acting like an amateur tap dancer. The situation isn't grave so John *could* get on a plane and return for a repeat performance with the U.S. cardiologist. He'd had the procedure once before and the cardiologist had warned that it just might not take. If he returned he could use the U.S. health insurance. However, just before leaving for France John's Atlanta cardiologist had provided the name of a *cardiologue* at the teaching hospital in Tours. He is the head *professeur* of *Hôpital Trousseau,* part of the university teaching system here. The hospital is excellent, highly regarded, and recommended for heart patients. Before hopping a plane we decide to get another opinion.

The doctor and hospital are only 30 minutes from the house. We'd never actually been to the hospital, so we need a better map of the city of Tours. This is the goal when I stop by the local *papeterie* in town. The stationary store had served as office to some extent since we'd been sending and receiving faxes there for months. Occasionally, I'd buy a new pen, or a postcard or two.

The store is small, but crammed with stationary, pens, wrapping paper, greeting cards, art supplies and books, including tour guides and maps. Beyond the shelves lined with French paperbacks, Madame Huart appears to be busy with another customer so I find the metal rack of maps and begin my search for Tours. After several minutes, I pick a map that looks promising. It doesn't show hospitals, just a maze of streets. The hospital, however, has to be on one of them.

The customer before me leaves. Madame Huart looks up from the counter filled with datebooks and decorative stamps and smiles a "*bonjour.*" I brave more conversation than usual and explain that my husband needs to find the hospital in Tours. I don't see it on the map but ...

She stops me. Mentioning hospital and need in the same sentence unleashes solicitude beyond expectations.

Madame waves the map I'd handed her and shakes her head vigorously. "*Non, non*, there is a better map for the streets. I will show you."

She exits her spot behind the counter and weaves through the aisles toward the map display, towing me behind her like a tug. *Madame* leafs through the maps on the rack that I'd just left. She mumbles something to herself, which I understand as meaning that what she is searching for isn't there. She bends down, opens a drawer and briefly rustles through it.

"I hope I did not sell it," she says. She stands up and looks on the revolving map display again. I peer over her shoulder and point at a spiral-bound map book of the region. Is that what she's looking for? "*Non.*" Madame moves to the tour guides, pulls some out and looks behind them. She gives up and returns to the drawer.

"I'm sure this map," I indicate the one I'd originally picked out, "will be fine."

"Non," she says. "That's not right."

"Ahhh, here it is." She pulls a map from the drawer and stands up. I hold out my hand to take the map and compare it to the one I'd decided on originally. This simple operation is becoming a long procedure. I just want a map, an inexpensive map, a map that will show me the streets of Tours.

174

Madame holds onto the map and spreads it out on top of the *Guides Michelin* on the middle shelf. I'm beginning to regret that I'd attempted the conversation. My Type A personality is still alive and kicking about the fact that I could have purchased a map and been gone on other errands before the shops closed at twelve-thirty.

"*Regardez, ici*," Madame calls my attention to the map. I'd started this. Now I am duty -bound to follow the scenario through to the finish.

"You are here." She points to Montrichard. "You go like this." Her finger traces a line along the route to Tours, south of the Cher, skips quickly over a few busy main roads and points. "There," is *Hôpital Trousseau*."

"That's good, *merci bien*," I say. "I'm sure we can find it now." Ahh, we can complete the sale now and I'll be on my way. But Madame makes no moves toward the cash register.

She asks if I know the back route. "Back route?"

"*Plus vite*," faster, she says, "for the hospital." Her finger starts from Montrichard and pauses halfway to Tours. "See, here, the small road." Her driving finger diverges from the national highway, winds scenically through vineyards and hamlets, and arrives smack-dab in front of the hospital.

"*C'est directe. Moins du traffic.*" She explains. "It's direct. Less traffic." She folds the map back in perfect rectangles and marches toward the counter. It becomes evident I don't have a choice. I will be getting the map she'd selected.

As she leads the way toward the cash register she seems so happy with herself that a shameful thought flashes through my mind. So shameful, I'm embarrassed to admit it. As I follow this sweet woman with soft gray curls and beaming smile, I have a sudden vision of a page from a marketing manual, with guiding rule number one being, "Move up the sale." I can't help but wonder if the map *Madame* had so conveniently found, the one that truly is a better indicator of the streets, is double the price of the one I'd originally chosen.

Under the solicitude of this *mère poule*, this mother hen, does there beat the heart of a *mère* merchandising expert?

I have to know. If I'd been had, so be it. If I hadn't, I'd forever know that Madame has my best interests at heart. I pay at the counter, all the while making my plan. I wander down the aisle to leave and surreptitiously glance at the map I'd originally chosen, searching for the price tag. Marketers of the world may shudder, but my faith in French humanity remains intact.

Madame's choice cost less.

* * *

The day arrived for John's appointment with the cardiologist. The map got us to the hospital at Tours efficiently and we were ten minutes early. We did some preliminary paperwork, sat in the waiting room for a few minutes, and were installed in a room with desk, bookshelves, and an examining table behind a partial wall. We chose chairs in front of the empty desk and waited.

An efficient knock, then a youth in a white coat walked in the door. He couldn't have been older than my daughter. My own heart skipped a beat. I hoped this wasn't the cardiologist.

No, this is an intern, one of the professor's students, sent to take the preliminaries, the blood pressure and an EKG. John hops on the table and I scan the office. Behind me, the bookshelves are filled with weighty tomes on heart and circulatory diseases. It is amazing how easily I can read the titles. Of course, half of them are written in English. Evidently French cardiologists keep up-to-date with the goings-on in English medical journals. The fact is comforting for the breadth of their knowledge. On the other hand, I hope these French doctors have a better working knowledge of English than we have of French.

176

I try not to consider that.

When the true *cardiologue* bustles in, he epitomizes confidence. The salt-and-pepper hair helps, along with the fact that he looks my husband directly in the eye and never wavers in his conviction. He can put the thump thump thump back into my husband's heart. So the procedure didn't take the first time in the states? Not to worry, this *cardiologue* knows the secret. He will prescribe the exact combination of *medicaments*, diet, and exercise that will prevent a relapse. John's heart would get its rhythm back permanently this time.

Of course, afterwards, John will have to give up wine but… What?

John looks at me in panic. Did the doctor really say what he just thought he said? I look at the doctor. I understood everything to this point. But this *had* to be a misunderstanding. A Frenchman who suggested giving up wine is inconceivable, un-natural, maybe even unpatriotic. Our confidence sinks. This man is obviously a quack.

The doctor explains. With John's history, he will need medication plus he must give up alcohol, which apparently can cause the heart, if predisposed to it, to go out of rhythm. Unless my husband wants to become addicted to electric wires, he'll have to limit his wine intake. Grudgingly, the doctor agrees that John could have half a glass -- but no more -- of wine a day.

On the drive home through the vineyards, we compare notes. If it had to be, it had to be.

"We can empty out the wine cave," I say.

"No," John replies. "I don't have to give up the collecting. I just don't have to drink it."

He could continue to visit the co-operative. He could merrily cork the bottles with that satisfying swoosh as they popped into place. He could label them and place each bottle lovingly into its slot -- reds on the right, whites in the middle, bubbly and port stacked on the left.

John would enjoy the wine *cave* by serving the wine to friends. He, himself, would stick to his half a glass.

***

John had spunk and he never complained about the sentence passed on him. He would brave a French world without wine. He'd brave the electric shock. The only thing he wasn't sure about was braving a French hospital with his poor French language skills. (Considering that his first and best French sentence ordered wine, this didn't serve him well under the circumstances.)

Nevertheless, my husband is a pillar of strength. We talk it over and in order to stay in France he will manage with the French hospital provided that I am there at all essential moments for translation, especially the day of the procedure. He wants to ensure that he isn't sent off for an appendectomy instead of the cardioversion.
***

John will be in the hospital three days. This is a shock in itself; the procedure is outpatient in the states. We mention this to the *cardiologue*. The same man who calmly announced that wine was a *non-non* sputters with emotion at the mention of outpatient treatment for the cardioversion. This epitome of medical expertise actually blanches.

"But how do they do the preparation and follow after?" he asks. "It must be three, maybe four days here."

We consider the price. We would be paying for this treatment in France and, hopefully, be reimbursed later by the insurer. Maybe. What would all this cost? Perhaps, if not outpatient, just one night?

The doctor recites the litany of services that his cardiology department will provide in a one-price-fits-all system. All doctors, including him, the head of the cardiology department, all nurses, pre- and post-testing, anesthesia, the procedure itself, and three days of delicious French meals (a bit exaggerated that).

178

"What will this cost?" We ask again.

He looks at us blankly since the universal health care system in France covers its citizens. He has no idea what it will cost if someone were to pay out-of-pocket.

We talk to the hospital billing office on the way out. The cost in dollars for the complete three days will be equivalent to $1,100.

We call the hospital in Atlanta and ask for an estimate for the outpatient procedure there. The number is almost the same. *If* you add another 0 to the end. At almost $11,000, the same procedure would cost ten times as much for the outpatient, shock, bam, thank you sir, service.

It becomes no-contest. John would have the procedure in Tours. Later, we contact our insurance company, which at first doesn't want to cover the procedure in France, but they agree. Considering that the price to them was a tenth of what they would have paid in the U.S. they should have thanked us profusely. Roughly speaking, John saved them almost $10,000

Perhaps they should export all their members to foreign countries.

***

The first night of John's hospital stay, I follow the routines. I walk Folly at ten o'clock as usual, but John isn't sitting in the living room when we leave. The streets are empty and we pick our way from streetlight to streetlight. We don't go far and return quickly. Folly gets extra cuddles – or he gives them to me. I'm not sure which.

He curls up at my feet. I try to read but sounds are amplified in the house. The water heater in the attic is making strange noises. I'll have to get it checked. Can water heaters overheat and blow up? Do they burst and create Niagara Falls down the stairs?

I think briefly of burglars and other bogeymen but I'm living in a fortress. The house sleeps soundly within thick stone walls. What isn't stone is barricaded, the result of the Madame the rose-lovers' fear when she lived alone after her husband died.

She had calmed her fears with triple locks, grates on lower windows and of course, our famous front gate. That gate with its pointed spikes was more convincing than the elaborate electronic burglar alarm in the states.

There is one thing that the walls couldn't protect me from. I wonder what I would do… if… That big 'if' that women with husbands anywhere over forty, even more, over sixty, can't help but consider on dark lonely nights when the next day their man is about to have high-voltage applied to his heart.

I head up the narrow stairs to commune with the Virgin Mary across the street. To be without John is a frightening thought. Especially in a country that isn't my own. Where I speak the language, but not as naturally as my own. The sharp points of my gate can't protect me from any of those fears. It occurs to me, however, that if the worst happened, I'd feel lost *wherever* I was.

The Madonna watches over me in a gentle fortress overlooking the Cher river. I sleep soundly until the six-thirty garbage pickup rouses me.

Click. Clack the morning's shutters are thrown open in the elemental ritual of dawn in France. I drive to Tours via Madame's shortcut. John gets his voltage cranked up at the hospital. His heart starts beating with an even thump thump thump thump.

Three days later, *le cardiologue* agrees John can leave the hospital. With gray brows knit together he pins John to the wall with his eyes. He delivers the stern reminders: Take the pills. Get gentle exercise. Don't drink.

John returns home. We celebrate his regular heartbeat with a sweet vintage from the vineyards. Grape juice.

28
LOTS OF NUTS

John heads for the back shed to pump up the bike tires. On the concrete apron just outside the shed door his feet skid over crunchy brown marbles. He looks closer. *Noisettes*, virtually the national nut of France, carpet the area. They roll like ball bearings wherever he disturbs them.

He looks up. Above are branches of a massive tree we have admired for its shade, height, and ability to hide the rear of a nursing home down the hill, preserving our privacy. The tree is hailing hazelnuts and the breeze helps push them off the branches. Some conk into his shoulder and he looks down again. A mass of nuts roll across the white concrete. He could pick these up but most of the branches spread over the shed's roof.

I wonder what's taking John so long with the bikes. By the time I get to the shed to hear the story, he's on a ladder harvesting nuts from the shed roof.

"You won't believe it," he says. "There are tons of hazelnuts up here." They'd been captured like minnows in a net, as they rolled down the shed roof and into the gutters. He harvests them in huge piles.

We have plastic grocery bags filled with the unexpected bounty. It is truly unexpected since we hadn't even recognized the tree as something that would dispense nuts. We are suddenly living with the earth's largesse. Like pioneers we intend to make the most of it.

John takes one grocery bag filled with nuts into the house and starts cracking.

The shelled hazelnuts become the *raison d'être* for our menu plans. We coat fresh cod with grated hazelnuts, we top pumpkin soup with crunchy chopped hazelnuts, and make brownies filled with whole hazelnuts. Several pans of them. Our chocolate fetish helped use them up and it was easier to use hazelnuts whole than have to chop them and grate them anyway.

Meanwhile, we're still harvesting hazel nuts from the gutters, which trap them handily. The wind picked up at night and every morning we reaped another bountiful bag full of them.

By now plastic bags filled with hazelnuts are piled along our small kitchen counter. We don't bother putting the nutcrackers back into the drawer. John begins a ritual of cracking hazelnuts every time he sits in front of television, a big bowl of them between his knees. He starts watching more television. Our hands are cramped with cracking and now plastic bags of *noisettes* take up the space in the lower compartment of the freezer.

I make more hazelnut brownies than even chocoholics like John and I can eat. I give away brownies. Except to make them we still have to crack the nuts. Eventually we mainline, offering straight-off-the-tree hazelnuts to every friend within ten kilometers. One accepted some. The rest have hazelnut trees themselves, have gone through this exercise before, and have already adjusted to superfluous nuts. They leave them on the ground.

Even that culinary great, Marie-France, shakes her head in regret. She understands the problem, but she and Michel have more than enough themselves. (She admits this after I'd plied her with hazelnut brownies. She'd never had a brownie before and despite the fact they were made with French hazelnuts, she considered it a "real American" recipe.) As for anything else, even Marie-France is at a loss as to know what to do with a half ton of hazelnuts. She can't can them or make them into *confiture*, though she does freeze some.

Hazelnuts continue to drop from the skies. "It's an especially good year for hazelnuts," she says. I have no means of comparison though I did live through Upstate New York snowfalls that were lighter than this.

Where the heck are squirrels when you need them?

182

***

When we weren't shoveling up hazelnuts, we were studying mushrooms. In the fall, they're easily found in the market. But the challenge is to get your mushrooms without paying for them. For that, the French turn into stealthy mushroom hunters.

John and I are leery of doing this ourselves. We're tempted, of course. The local pharmacies even encourage us. Their windows display plastic mushrooms in cardboard forests. Up front and center is a poster displaying the countless types of mushrooms, ranging from the delicious *chanterelles* and *girolles* that you can eat joyfully, to the ones that will, *malheureusement*, kill you. In between the two are pictures of the ones that just will make you sick enough to wish they would.

We peruse the poster and notice mushrooms chillingly named *Trompettes de Mort* – death trumpets. They're dark as midnight, slimy, and shaped like what could conceivably be considered Gabriel's horn. Just when we're sure we at least can recognize one deadly mushroom, we note that the poster lists them as edible.

We weren't about to take the chance that it was a typographic error. We see people entering the pharmacy with baskets of mushrooms. The pharmacist is trained to separate the edible from the deadly and will help out when called for. We consider that. But we also note the busy pharmacy and wonder if the pharmacist is not a tad too busy to be trusted with separating the good, bad and the plain ugly. We never quite get up the nerve to go picking and resign ourselves to the market mushrooms.

British friends, Starr and Doug, are braver. I assume it's because they've been brought up in the arts of mushroom gathering. They were walking their dog, Florence, one bright fall day when they happened upon a mushroom area of enormous potential. It was, to hear them tell it, a veritable minefield of succulent mushrooms. They hadn't come prepared with baskets but they filled their jacket pockets and put whatever they could in their hands. As they strolled home they planned the evening's mushroom menu, and resolved to return early the next day with baskets.

They nodded "*bonjour*" to a neighbor as they passed him.

Bright and early the next morning they returned with baskets, dreaming of mushroom soup, mushroom omelets, mushroom quiches, and buttery, sautéed mushrooms with *steak au poivre*.

They reached the field and started searching. This was the place, they were sure of it. Had they been dreaming? Nary a mushroom could be found.

Then they remember their mistake. The evening before they had passed their neighbor, their hands filled with mushrooms. They should have taken a lesson from the French book and adopted evasive maneuvers.

I recall a sign in the forest near Chaumont where we bike. Beside the edge of the road it warns, "No mushroom hunting. Traps." Some French will go to any lengths to guard their mushrooms. We always wondered if the owner of the property had seriously placed traps for unscrupulous mushroom hunters, or do they think the threat is enough, bringing to mind as it does, steel jaws in a bear trap. Knowing the French attitude toward mushrooms, we're not taking the chance.

29
GOURMANDISE

Dining out is one of the chief pleasures of living in France. It's greatly enhanced by time and money.

As early retirees, time is something we have plenty of.

As early retirees, money is another story.

But we happened to be on a visit to the gastronomic city of Lyon, known far and wide, mostly wide, for offering more magnificent calories per square kilometer than almost any place else in France.

At lunch time we were within a toothpick's throw of one of *haute cuisine*'s legendary temples: Paul Bocuse. A dear friend and part of a food-loving couple had dined there on a trip to France and insisted that it was an experience beyond anything we would experience. She would never forgive us if we didn't try it. "Just once," she said. "Sure, it's expensive, but you only live once." We liked the philosophy. It was our bank account that didn't like the idea.

Curiosity and hunger are an irresistible combination. We rationalized that we could afford this luxury for lunch. Lunch is never as expensive as dinner. Right? Even at Paul Bocuse, or so we thought.

The restaurant was located several kilometers outside Lyon proper, at Collonges-au-Mont-d'Or. We found a phone and dialed the number.

Yes, the restaurant was open. Yes, it had a table for two. We hung up and checked our wallets. Yes, we would charge it.

Outside it was a blistering summer day. Inside, the temperature cooled with *sang-froid* and our self-consciousness. We had spiffed up as well as we could for the occasion but our traveling clothes had suffered during the previous hours behind the wheel. It can't be helped. We shrug and trot after the *maitre d'* to reach the table as quickly as possible. Behind the long white linen tablecloths, who could tell the wrinkles, really?

The chief chef of Lyon is known for his signature *soupe au truffes* -- truffle soup. This specialty is one reason the Michelin Guide puts the restaurant in the category of "worth a special trip." We're here already so we intend to take full advantage.

Knowing that truffles are known as 'black gold,' we expect to pay through the bowl. And when we see the price of roughly $30 for that bowl we wonder if we get to keep the china. We also wonder if the friend who had insisted we dine here is connected with the Colombian drug cartels or keeping her lottery winnings a secret.

However, this would undoubtedly be the only chance we'd have to live like the rich and famous, so we do what any other cheap-but-curious-for-a-taste couple would do in the situation. We order one bowl.

It's put in front of me, mainly because my husband is less concerned with minor details of etiquette involved in reaching over a table to steal from another plate. The soup arrives with a thick crust billowing above the bowl. The truffle treasure is hidden beneath. I tap the crust with a spoon on one corner and sample the soup. My champion taster, John, is champing at the bit for his turn so I slide the bowl slightly towards him. We know "sharing" like common eaters would just not do in a bastion of *haute cuisine* so John slips his spoon over for periodic surreptitious slurps while I stand lookout, ensuring that the waiter doesn't calling the etiquette police.

While keeping lookout, I sneak peaks at the next table across the aisle. A silver-haired, just-coifed matron is guiding three young, be-suited men through the challenges of the gourmet menu. I imagine her to be a duchess or chatelaine of a nearby vineyard with her retinue. Whoever, she is not a neophyte to this bastion of *haute cuisine.* Paul Bocuse himself abandons the kitchen in order to offer that table his *bonjour* as well as free champagne.

I pat down my hair and check to see if truffle soup has spilled on my shirt.

The rest of the dinner passed pleasantly enough. After the soup came the main courses. To say I had the lamb and John had salmon would be like comparing preschool art to Michelangelo. The plates looked better than we did.

The cheese course was over the top, with at least two dozen choices rolled to the table. I wanted to request one of each. Unfortunately, I'd learned cheesy manners from our French friends. Most of them politely limit themselves to two, perhaps three selections at the most. I thought of the price of the menu. John thought of the tastes he'd be missing.

It was excruciating to limit ourselves. (John cheated and tried four.)

I was saving myself anyway. The best was still to come: Dessert.

Dessert had been mentioned on the menu but not in detail. All we know is that it is '*compris*,' that is, included. The exact nature of the treat is a mystery.

The server used his silver crumb picker-upper device deftly to prepare the linen tablecloth as though a sacred altar. He left us to imagine the possibilities and build suspense.

He returned and ceremoniously placed a small silver plate filled with glossy dark chocolate-covered almonds in the center of the table. Next to it he added a silver platter lined end-to-end with thin oval cookies, crisp, buttery, and coated on top with a layer of deep rich chocolate. Hershey's, it wasn't.

In front of each of us, he placed a shallow round dish of *crème brulée.* The rich custard was perfectly browned, where the chef had used his gourmet flamethrower to burn the top to crisp, caramelized perfection.

We finished the *crème brulée.* We worked at the cookies and the chocolate-covered almonds. We nibbled "just one more taste, it's soooo good." Soon every plate was as clean as Folly's dog dish the day we treated him to liver paté. Sated with pleasure we sat back to do a play-by-play of the meal and await a stomach-settling coffee.

That's when the waiter brought the dessert cart.

Apparently, our three prior sweets were designed merely to tease the appetite -- like a series of *hors d'oeuvres* -- for the real desserts. The serious sweets appeared on a rolling trolley of two levels, which presented several different pies and cakes, bowls of puddings, and a heaping bowl of whipped cream for garnishing anything you wanted garnished. It was the adult version of *Willy Wonka and the Chocolate Factory.*

Our eyes bulged. Our buttons popped. These wonders were already included in the king's ransom we were paying for one lunch, how could we say no?

We didn't.

***

In Montrichard we settle for our usual gastronomy. Delicious but simpler and less extravagant. We visited Madame for more French lessons and, as usual, the discussion headed toward any topic Madame wanted. It was on this occasion, food.

The trade war between the U.S. and France was heating up. The European Union didn't want hormone-treated beef or genetically-modified food to be allowed into the region. France was even more horrified at the thought.

The United States was determined. They wanted the free market and if they couldn't sell their hormones in France, the United States would tax all the good stuff imported from France. They put champagne and Roquefort cheese and *foie gras* on the list.

As I read the newspaper and discussed this with Madame, it seemed that my country was doing more to hurt Americans than the French. Our fellow citizens in the states were suffering without these goodies or paying ten times what we were paying for them on the other side of the Atlantic.

188

France and the EU were standing pat. We were cheering for the French on this one. We'd been fortunate enough to discover what truly fresh fruits and vegetables taste like and opening the floodgates to doctored designer foods wasn't in our plans.

Madame was preaching to the converted the day she expounded on the problem with cheeses. "The U.S. won't allow us to send them unpasteurized cheeses," she fumed. "But that's what makes our cheeses good."

Her logic was succinct. "So why do they want to import our cheeses, but make us change them to make them not taste good?"

***

Some French decided to protest in front of that paragon of American gourmandise: McDonald's. But, of course, the owners of the chain were usually French. Thus, they were caught in the middle. One McDonald's franchisee decided to show his solidarity with the French cause.

He made his Big Macs, all right. He served them with onion, pickles, tomato, on a sesame seed bun.

But he made them with *foie gras*.

30
MISSING PARTS

We planned a quick two-week visit to the states. Folly was getting up there in years and his heart was giving him problems so we decided to leave him with Nadia during our absence. Though he was a good traveler, two weeks was too short a time to make him endure the hours in the airline doggy carrier. Nadia would take good care of him. She'd give him his medicine and lipstick kisses. He could run happily around the courtyard as much as his little legs and aging heart would allow.

We got up at five a.m. to leave from our local train station. We'd transfer in St. Pierre de Corps to the fast TGV train that goes directly to Charles DeGaulle airport north of Paris. The house was shuttered tight from the night before. We added a few last-minute items to the luggage. We removed the last-minute items that wouldn't fit.

By six a.m. we had checked that the coffee pot was unplugged, gathered the keys, and pulled the folding steel grate across the patio and entry doors. It was the official vacation lock-down *a la* Alcatraz.

It was still dark and we fumbled with luggage and keys. Just then it began to rain. Hard. We dragged our suitcases out the front gate and paused. Our faithful Citroën was gleaming under the street light. We had planned to walk the two blocks to the train station, leaving the car in front of the house. But now it's raining and dark. Surely, the car can survive just two weeks parked at the station. We are a tad unnerved by the idea of leaving the car there, still, what is the difference, we ask each other, if the car sits at the station two blocks away or outside our town house? The difference was that we wouldn't get soaked.

As we park outside the station, I comment gaily to John how fortunate we are to find the first space free, directly under the lights. Our car would be safe. It would be in full view. It sure was.

Two weeks later, we returned home.

"I'll take the cases to the other exit," says John. "You go get the car and pull it around."

"Ok," I agree.

I mount the steps to the footbridge that crosses the tracks, which provides a birds-eye view of the parking lot. I can't see our car. I tell myself there must be a truck in the way. In the lot, I walk down the line of cars where we'd parked. That's strange, I can't see it from here either. I keep walking. I walk past the first parking spot. The one directly under the lamp post. I look again. That parking spot has a car in it all right, but it isn't ours. My memory might not be the greatest but I didn't think I'd forget what the Citroën looked like in just two weeks. Darn. Maybe the station doesn't allow long-term parking and we'd been towed.

I head for the station building to find out how to ransom our vehicle. The clerk today is a stolid, practical woman we know from countless ticket-buying. I ask her if someone towed our car. Who would we contact to get it back? I am wondering how much towing charge we'll have to pay.

"Are you sure it is not there?" She asks me.

Alarm bells rang in my head.

"You must report it," she adds.

"Yes, naturally," I reply.

"How long has it been missing?" she asks.

"Ummm, that's the problem. I don't know." I'm ashamed to admit we had left our faithful vehicle for two weeks. "But it was under the light," I say.

"Very clearly there, then."

"Yes, very clearly." Very obviously, I might have added.

191

John had no clue what was taking me so long to pick him up at the corner. By the time I reached him, I'd reached full panic. Not for the car, for the house. Between the station and the corner where John waited, I realized that the car contained our insurance papers and tax papers, all required by French government. All showing our address. It would have been an easy step for the thieves to note the address and, since the car was "very clearly" left at the train station by people gone bye-bye, had used the opportunity to break in. We ran for home, as much as anyone can run with suitcases thumping along a bumpy road.

We impatiently unlocked the front gate, then struggled to unlock the Alcatraz grate covering the door. That was a good sign, though we couldn't see the back of the house to know if anything was disturbed there.

We scurried through the house, glancing right and left at double-time. Nothing seemed out of order. We calmed down. If the only thing lost was the Citroën, which was old and insured, we could handle it. Sorry, old friend. I felt a little guilty at considering our buddy disposable.

We were tired, we were jet-lagged, but the house was ok. Nevertheless, we must report the car to *les gendarmes*, then take ourselves to the insurance company. Meanwhile, we were car-less. We didn't know how long the car had been missing, but jet lag or no we had to report the missing car immediately. We trudged the four blocks uphill to the *gendarmerie*, reviewing in our minds the words for theft and the explanation that we'd need to supply. We were proud of our efforts to see justice done though every bone ached and our heads were muddled with the effects of an eight-hour flight in cattle class, two hours back via train, and the stress of trotting up the street, sure that someone had absconded with our house. It was noon and we were hungry but we could eat after we'd done our civic duty and reported the theft.

We rounded the curve up the hill and reached the front gate of the *gendarmerie*. The gate has a self-locking system. You ring the bell and after you state your business the police inside unlock the door. We held the gate handle to pull it open as soon as the police clicked us in. The speaker stuttered, asking what we wanted.

"Our car has been stolen," we reported.

"Come back at two," said the disembodied voice.

The *gendarmerie* was closed for lunch. Obviously, even French criminals are expected to dine from noon to two.

***

I was unpacking the suitcases at six o'clock that evening when the phone rang.

"*Madame Kuh-norrrr?*"

It was the police in Orléans, 100 kilometers away.

"You reported your car is missing?"

Oui, I had reported it that afternoon. The policeman explained that our car had been heisted for a heist. A jewelry store. Then the car was abandoned. They had wondered to whom it belonged. There had been no missing car reports matching the vehicle. Until that afternoon, that is.

"We were away for two weeks," I said, feeling like a fool for the third time today. I had admitted committing the same naïve error of car neglect to the clerk at the train station, the gendarmes, and now the Orléans police.

The next day we borrowed a vehicle from Jacky at the garage and drove to the Orléans police department. The young policeman was polite. He shook hands, led us through a maze of corridors to one room, changed rooms when he was dissatisfied with the first one, and then re-appeared with his personal notebook computer to make out the report. We explained the whole sordid mess and he explained how our vehicle had been apprehended after its foray into the world of jewel

193

robbery. He told us where to find the police lot. We could pay a condolence visit to the suspect *Citroën*. It was in sad shape thanks to its outlaw activities. The whole car had only been $3,000 when we purchased it three years ago. Now it looked like something that had been the bad guy in a Jackie Chan movie.

Were John and I dismayed? If truth be told, we both had the same thought: insurance money! We had been considering a new car to make our European jaunts more secure. We had our eyes on a used Renault that had only been driven by a little old man on his way to *boules* tournaments every Saturday. Could the robbers have done us a favor? The insurance money might be better than anything we'd get for the *Citroën*. If we'd thought of this we might have even issued an invitation.

Trying to stop grinning ear to ear, we visited our insurance representative to report the state of the car.

"We'll repair it," said the insurance representative.

"You don't have to." John and I fell over each other replying. "We're sure it's not worth repairing."

"That's our policy."

"Couldn't you just give us the same amount in cash instead?"

We got a blank look. Fixing up is the rule, whatever it costs. It cost a lot. Not enough for a new car, but a hefty chunk of it.

Our delinquent vehicle returned to us five weeks later.

***

Two months later we bought the Renault. The Citroën became the "family truck" and hauled the gardening supplies and anything too messy for the Renault. The Citroën lasted another few months before the transmission went. We hoped it was related to its adventures as a getaway car. It wasn't. The insurance company had repaired and returned the car. It hadn't factored in the fact that the car was ready to give up its ghostly gaskets at any moment.

We returned to being a one-car couple with just the Renault. It got us to Spain on a June vacation. (Well, we called it a vacation. My daughter got technical on that point since a vacation is what people take who have a chance to get away from work. Ok, so it was a trip.) We returned too late to make it to the Friday market and John took the Renault to the local grocery store to grab a few things. It was a busy Saturday afternoon, the parking lot was packed with people. He went shopping, came out in fifteen minutes. The hubcaps were missing. He rounded the car. All four hubcaps were missing.

"Gypsies," said Michel.

"Gypsies," said Marie-France.

"Gypsies," said Annick.

"Ghosts," I said. "They had to be. The parking lot was the busiest it ever is that day. How could anyone swipe four hubcaps one after the other? In fifteen minutes."

"They can do it, *vite*."

They had a point. Whoever took them, the hubcaps were there and then they weren't. The insurance company wouldn't cover them.

We visited the Renault dealer and got replacements. Five days later John walked outside. The hubcaps were missing. He rounded the car. Four hubcaps were missing.

We told Marie-France and Michel again. This time they weren't so sure about the gypsy connection. "Someone bought a Renault and needed the parts," said Michel. "It's the new thing. They're selling that model stripped down. But the owners want to fix it up. They now have a real market in hubcaps. Even back seats."

"We checked. The back seat is still there."

"No matter. If you buy new hubcaps, the real Renault hubcaps, they will steal them again. Buy the cheap hubcaps at the mall. Not Renault," said Michel. "You will not have the problem. No one will steal them."

We did. They didn't.

31
AU REVOIR, TRISTESSE

The skies are a sodden gray quilt. The town has smothered under its weight for nine weeks in a row, give or take what John calls a 'sucker' hole from his Air Force days. The sun peaks out for half an hour, just enough to give us hope that the weather will soon cheer up. We want to walk along the river path but the mud is inches deep. We want to ride our bikes through the vineyards but we'd float off into the sunset. We want to clear out the ivy in the garden. It's the only thing that seems to be thriving despite the damp, depressing days.

Each day our hopes are dashed. We go to bed at night and wake up groggy. We're sure that it must be five in the morning, only to discover that it's already nine a.m. The darkness has encouraged us to continue dreaming. Why not? we tell each other, considering the dismal weather.

According to *le journal*, the past winter and early spring have been the worst for rain and raw temperatures since 1961. The France 2 weather woman agrees, though judging from her radiant smile, she's not disturbed by the news. Why should she be? She has all of Paris to enjoy museums, galleries and shops – *indoor* activities -- while we're here in the countryside where we're meant to be hiking and biking and strolling the outdoor markets.

Meanwhile, we're watching her and learning the French terms for rain, hail, fog and sleet. We're trapped in the house and I start to think about bookstores with cozy coffee shops where one can while away dreary days reading magazines. Except French country villages are noticeably lacking in mega-bookstores -- especially any that serve cappuccino while you peruse row upon row of free magazines.

John is content painting in his atelier. I get restless and grumble. Eventually I gather up my raincoat and umbrella and head for town to splurge on *croissants.* The *boulangerie* at the end of our street makes melt-in-your-mouth croissants with real butter. If you're getting calories anyway, you may as well enjoy them. And real butter croissants are supremely better than anything made with vegetable shortening. The French agree. At least, they agree that people should know what they're buying – and paying for, since the butter croissants cost more. The government legislates the appearance of croissants so that no one can pull a fast one, claiming a croissant is pure and flaky butter-made while using vegetable oil. The true croissant is triangular with the points straight across. If the points are curved then they're not the real thing.

On normal Sunday mornings, the straight buttery version is rich enough to send our taste buds to heaven and our cholesterol reeling. Under the depressing clouds we plan to overdose.

John's favorite is stuffed with almond paste and covered with sliced toasted almonds. I head for the almond paste, with chocolate. Anything chocolate. We will take them home, make our own coffee, and, instead of Barnes and Noble, we'll read the latest contributions ordered via www.amazon.co.uk.

Just the thought of the treat in store raises my spirits. I'm heading down the street while my neighbor from three doors down is coming back up. From the looks of the soggy baguette stuffed into one deep raincoat pocket, she's returning from the same destination. She gestures toward the dirty linen above and pronounces it "*gris*" or grey. I nod in agreement. The weather is easily translated.

The *boulangerie* the warm smell of fresh breads provides some comfort, though it's a challenge to avoid spraying umbrella drippings over the bread counter. I shake the umbrella carefully outside and place it by the door before making my order. Meanwhile, Madame, the baker's wife, clarifies the day as "*moche.*" Loosely translated, it's "ugly."

That afternoon, at the hairdresser's for a *coupe*, I comment on the gray skies, and Mademoiselle, the *coiffeuse*, looks heaven-ward, somberly pronouncing that it's "*triste.*" Sad, it is. A strange commentary on the weather but the term gathers force. It becomes the most common term I hear as the leaden clouds imprison the sun. And us.

The weather has cast a pall on life, putting our region in the running as the test lab for seasonal affective disorder.

This is no way to spend a spring. We need to rouse ourselves. Fortunately, there are compensations when one retires in the Loire.

It's called lunch. Nothing cures *triste* nearly as well as a spirit-lifting, five-courses with wine – preferably a meal that takes not just the requisite two hours, but four or five if one is fortunate to share the table with effusive friends.

It's even better if those effusive friends are generous with their wine cave. Such is the case with a British couple nearby whose favorite hobbies, fortunately for their friends, are cooking and collecting wines. Lunch is cheery with them. And they hold the record for lengthy ones. English-speaking category, that is. The French category is unattainable unless you're born French.

In any case, our English world record occurred after five weeks of straight rain. It cleared one day and grew mild. It was an opportunity for a *déjeuner* à *l'herbe*. Starr and Doug called. Would we care to have lunch Monday noon? That happened to be the day for John's French lesson, which begins at three o'clock. No problem, three hours seemed sufficient to us. OK, as luncheon guests in the Loire, we were still on our learning permits.

We arrived promptly and joined the other guests, another British couple, with a glass of wine. There was absolutely nothing more pressing to anyone else at the table than excellent company, a five-course menu created by people for whom good food is an art form, and a different wine with each course. We were solving every problem in the American, British and French universes.

198

By three o'clock we were waiting for the cheese tray. Doug was scouting in his cellar for a nice red to try with it.

Everyone relaxed in their lawn chairs, pacing themselves. We have all day. A sunny one at that. We are making up for lost time by not rushing.

John, who couldn't drink more than his half glass had cheated by a few halves, but not by enough to forget his duty. He is due at Madame's for his French lesson at four p.m.

At 3:45 he turns to me and whispers, "What should I do? I can't just leave lunch. It's not polite." Besides, they hadn't served John's favorite course yet, dessert.

He considers calling Madame and canceling the lesson. The problem is that Madame's phone number is red-listed. The operator wouldn't give it out. We have Madame's number back at the house, but not with us. So John can't simply call her.

At ten to four John nervously looks at his watch for the tenth time. At five to four John stands up and announces that he has to make a visit. He heads up the wide steps from Starr and Doug's garden into their house. I don't know what kind of visit everyone else thought he was making, but I knew what he's up to. When he reached the front door, he sprinted for the car, drove the six blocks to Madame's house, rang the bell, got buzzed in, and after a hurried greeting, explained the problem. He was having *le dejeuner* with friends. It was taking longer than he thought. They were just starting the cheese course.

John appeared back at the table in fifteen minutes. Madame understood completely. He explained to me later that she had been completely *d'accord.*

"Of course, it is only natural." she'd told him. "You must have the cheese, dessert, and coffee. Come back tomorrow."

She understood. So did we, when we left Starr and Doug's lunch at five thirty that evening.

***

199

Three recent widows are part of our social group. All are involved and invited to events with the couples. There is no requisite pairing off or segregation. Many a dinner party was short two or three men and the only requisite of the diners was to spice up the conversation. The warmth evident in this small town, without the "couples only" mentality mitigates the *tristesse* with the warmth of human contact.

Odile is a stolid 60-something, and unlike the other widows, she's delighted with newfound freedom. Her reclusive husband had disliked entertaining. She's making up for lost time.

But her hip started hurting to the point where she couldn't walk or even sit comfortably. She needed *une intervention chirurgicale* and would spend two weeks in the hospital, then two months in a clinic. Even after our experience with John's heart, we're amazed at the length of time. But this is France, not the U.S., where undoubtedly the same procedure would be done on an outpatient basis of three hours, two if the HMO was particularly crafty.

Our French friends accept the long stay as perfectly normal. Since Odile has reached a certain age, and lives alone in a house with two sets of stairs, the doctors insist that she be pampered and spend clinic time gathering the strength to negotiate her home alone.

Annick telephoned one day. "We're going to visit Odile at the *clinique* today. Can you come?"

Bien sûr.

She'll call to arrange the time. "I need to coordinate," she says.

Ah, I understand. "Of course, in the states they limit visitors to no more than two visitors at a time."

"No, I need to coordinate with the other visitors," said Annick.

Marie-France and Pieta will go with us. That makes four, which fills up the car. It's possible that many more people will visit. Odile has many friends. Annick just wants to coordinate so we can see

Odile, just the four of us She would plan and orchestrate to avoid a *clinique* traffic jam.

Despite the preparations, there's been a miscommunication. We arrive at Odile's room and peek in the door. Odile is sitting up in bed. She's surrounded by flowers on a phone table, a side table, and a vase of them on the floor near the window. She and three friends are chatting and gesticulating with fervor. She looks for all the world like the queen holding court.

We enter, which only increases the hubbub while the group, now doubled in size exchange *bisous*, introductions, and handshakes. Annick has brought a covered basket with her. She discretely places under a narrow table in a corner of the room. We began chatting and fifteen minutes later two couples arrived together. Twelve people were jammed into the room, making maneuvering difficult. In an aside, Annick complains that they were supposed to come earlier but now they're late.

I'm trained to a system of three people and you've struck out of a hospital room into the corridor. In this case we're standing on the three sides of Odile's bed, with Annick occasionally maneuvering herself strategically onto the room's narrow balcony for a smoke.

The noise level was consistent with a mid-size cocktail party, which the group is beginning to resemble. I'm wondering just when it is we'll all get thrown out. I happen to be on the far side of the room, near the balcony, facing the entry door. Occasionally a hint of a white uniform passes by in the corridor. Finally, it happens. The nurse enters the doorway. She stands there a moment, views the scene. She says nothing. She leaves.

Eventually, the first two couples left. Now we're back to eight again. We can actually move about the room. Annick looks restless and mumbles something to me, about waiting out the newcomers who arrived after we did.

I look at my watch. Two hours have passed. It's beginning to look as though a clinic visit takes as long as a French lunch. The group chats. I lose a lot of the conversation, either because I don't know the people, places or events that they're chatting about, or I simply don't know the language.

Annick headed to the balcony for another cigarette. One of the other visitors mentions that it's getting cold with the balcony door open so we shut it. In another half hour they say goodbye, which takes fifteen minutes and leave.

Quiet descends. Marie France and Pieta looked at Annick in anticipation. Apparently they knew something I didn't. Annick drags the *panier* from under the table and places it next to the bed, on the side *away* from the corridor door. She opens it and pulls out a bottle of champagne.

"I couldn't open this before," she apologized. "There wasn't enough for twelve."

My mouth opened, but not for drinking. Do they really allow this in a clinic? I didn't want to ask, lest I convey my American ignorance on the drinking habits of the French. Annick struggled with the cork and winced when it made an unmistakable 'pop.' Co-conspirators, Marie-France and Pieta, giggled. Would the nurse hear? Did nurses even care in France? I got the distinct feeling that, even in France, champagne in the clinic might be frowned upon. The feeling intensified when Annick brazenly pulled five wine glasses from the basket. There was a perfectly good table next to Odile's bed, which would serve as a bar if we cleared off the tissues and water bottle. But even she wasn't about to push the rules too far. To pour the fizzy liquid, she placed the wine glasses on the floor behind the bed, on the opposite side from the door.

Definitely all is not completely freewheeling. When we heard the nurse's footsteps on the tile floor outside the room, Annick stopped pouring and thrust the open bottle into her basket with one hand and grabbed her purse with the other hand to cover it. She looked up, eyes widely innocent as the nurse poked her head in.

The low-key giggles that had followed the popping of the cork stopped in guilty silence. The nurse regarded the scene from the doorway. Our eyes darted to Annick who was clasping the neck of the guilty bottle to keep it upright, while hiding its rear portion in her *panier*.

Then she hiccupped.

The nurse headed imperiously toward the bed. She could not have missed Annick's wine glass still in view on the floor. (The others were behind our respective, if not respectable, backs.) I was sure that this staid representative of French nursing officialdom would condemn our actions, toasting us roundly for our toast to Odile. Would she send us and *panier* packing. Would she betray us to the administration? Would she at least aid Annick in stopping her hiccups?

Nope. She took Odile's temperature and left.

32

FRANCO-AMERICAN TWINS

Several gallons of French wine had passed our lips but those lips still mangled irregular French verbs with pitiful regularity. Nevertheless we two Americans were about to become French ambassadors to Germany.

It began with a phone call from Annick.

"I'm going to Eltville in Germany for the weekend," she says.

"How nice. Have a good trip."

"It's the *jumelage*."

"How nice." *Jumelage*? Is that a pilgrimage? I'd heard of those in France. No, that's *pelerinage*. Psst, quick, John, look up *jumelage*.

"Do you want to go?"

If it's anything like a *pelerinage*, I am already thinking of a polite excuse. But I can't imagine Annick as a pilgrim to anything other than a beach or casino.

Speaking slowly, Annick explains that *jumelage* is essentially a European twin city campaign, whereby a city in one country, France, twinned with a city in another, Germany, to promote friendship and cultural understanding. *Good idea*, I think. *Considering Europe's past history.*

The truth comes out. This year's visit to the twin city, Eltville, is in a pickle. Monsieur the President of the *jumelage* committee planned months in advance to participate in the German twin's Wine and Roses festival the first week in July. However, it's two weeks before takeoff and only three-quarters of the seats would have people sitting in them.

The group can't afford to lease the bus without a full complement of local residents as exchangees. And if the bus doesn't take the people who have already signed up, then they'd each have to drive the eight hours. That would lessen the attendance even further.

The social solidarity of the group would be shattered. The integrity of the association would be called into question. And who would join the German friends in Eltville to drink all their wine?

This, continues Annick, was why she called. Monsieur the President had urged the human grapevine to spring into action. Each person already signed up for the bus should spread the word about the trip and solicit bodies to fill the bus. They had a stake in it, after all, since their seats on the bus were on the line.

Our link to the grapevine is, of course, on the other end of the line. Annick has our number in more ways than one. She appeals to our taste for, not just wine, but cheap adventure in Europe.

"For $60 you can have four days in Germany at the Wine and Roses Festival in Eltville on the Rhine river. *Tout compris*, all included."

We understand wine and *tout compris*. Certainly enough to whet the thirst for more information. Had we heard correctly?

"You're kidding," I say. (It always helps to clarify clearly when dealing with money and a second language.)

"*Non, non. C'est vrai.*"

To hear Annick put it, for the aforementioned $60 each John and I could visit an area of Germany we'd never been, be transported there without paying the usual $4.50 a gallon of gas, lodge with German hosts, thereby getting a view of the country through insider's eyes, and be treated to dinners and entertainment all weekend.

(Naturally, no one mentioned that the entertainment would largely consist of sixteen speeches given in four days by twelve long-winded politicians or also-rans, each of which was translated sloooowly from French to German, or German to French, neither of which we were proficient in. But I digress.)

Two weeks later John and I yawn ourselves out of bed in the dark, still-shuttered bedroom. The wheels of our rolling bags clatter down the bumpy cobblestones, a wild strafing sound that disturbs that otherwise tranquil hour of 5:45 a.m. We hope that the tight shutters on the houses around us will cushion our neighbors' ears in their sleep.

At the end of the street we turn left past the *boulangerie* on the corner and the smell of freshly baked croissants tempts us to detour. We've lived in France long enough to resist two out of three times and this is one of them. We are eager to get to the assigned meeting place.

Up the hill and around the curve, the hulking shape of a modern *autocar,* the bus, sits under a streetlight, with people-shaped shadows flitting around it like moths. On its side, it advertises modern air conditioning and toilet facilities. Appropriately, it's parked directly in front of the small supermarket named in French a pantry, in other words it was called *Comode* – one reason that this particular supermarket seems particularly unappealing to us English speakers.

We present our baggage to the driver for loading in the shiny beast's belly. With it is included the *jumelage* committee's suggested three-pack of local sparkling wine as a hostess gift, which looks like everyone else's three-pack of local sparkling wine.

"How will we find which one is ours?" I ask.

"Does it matter?" replies John.

We mingle with the few friends we know and they introduce us to some new people. We provide cheeks to be kissed and hands to be shook. We look around for Annick. Some mutual friends ask if we have seen her. No one has. Perhaps she's around the other side of the bus? We make the tour. No Annick. In the public bathrooms on the corner perhaps? The *Comode* on the square wasn't open yet.

We wait ten minutes, make another tour around the clusters of people, looking closely for her slight figure and blond head behind larger shapes. Nope. Not there. She knows the correct time. After all, she's the one who recruited us.

On the dot of six a.m. *Monsieur*, the Committee President, requests that everyone settle themselves in seats. Our loyal cadre of friends saves a seat for Annick. Meanwhile all eyes are peering through the windows, watching anxiously for Annick to arrive. All mouths are making suppositions on what could have happened. What should we do? Is she all right? We all feel protective of little Annick. Widowhood has been rough on her. She's lively but lonely. Her friends have adopted her and none of us want to leave without knowing she's all right.

The bus vibrates as it starts. We're ready to pull out. *Monsieur*, the Committee President, is the *responsible* for the voyage. He's a dignified and efficient leader who notes the empty spot, counts heads, and asks where Annick is. We shake our heads. No one knows. *Monsieur*'s salt and pepper eyebrows knit together. He confers with the driver. "We must leave on schedule," he says.

We are getting nervous. This young widow, we knew, has been looking forward to the trip. No question of her forgetting. She had reminded *us*, for heaven's sake. And since her husband's death she is always eager to be with friends. We know that she doesn't want to spend the weekend alone.

Monsieur, the Committee President, uses his authority to hold the bus an extra ten minutes but his frown deepens.

No Annick.

The bus driver points to his watch. We glare at him and beg for a little more time. Perhaps she had a flat tire on the road. Could she have overslept?

Monsieur the Committee President finds Annick's phone number, borrows a cell phone, and calls her home. No answer. Ahh, she must be *en route*. Her house is only ten minutes away.

The bus waits another fifteen minutes. The driver is pacing back and forth outside the windows. We a leaving late, which would, we later discover, drastically cut our allotted two-hour lunch stop to just an hour and a half.

All attempts at finding Annick prove fruitless. *Monsieur*, the Committee President, calls someone staying in town to ask them to check on Annick. They promise to ensure she's all right and they will pass on the word that she can still get to Eltville with a couple who will be driving down independently the next day. Today is Friday. They couldn't close their fish store.

The next evening Annick appears at the dinner event with the couple.
She spends the rest of the weekend with a red face as the news spreads around the busload of concerned friends and townspeople.

Annick, our darling friend and lonely widow had indeed slept late. And not alone.

***

Based on the departure and arrival times our bus ride appeared to be an onerous ten hours. We had dreaded that part of the trip, assuming that the ten hours would be *travel* time, sitting cramped in a bus seat. This was a human error due to our American view of travel, which is to get on the *autoroute*, drive, stop at a drive-through, junk food eatery, use the facilities, and go. We should have known the French would not put themselves through such torture.

The bus stops for coffee at nine-thirty for half an hour. At noon we pull into the *autoroute* rest stop. *Monsieur*, the Committee President, announces lunch and everyone is told to be back to the bus no later than one-thirty because we have to make up time. We are sure we misheard. We ask again how long we would have. We don't want to miss the bus, after all.

Nope. We'd heard right. The leader is very sorry that we have to "rush" but we'd lost time at departure. Nevertheless we will stop here in the middle of the French high-speed *autoroute* for a proper hour-and-a-half lunch. Oh, sure, there is a faster cafeteria option. But as our friends point out, why would we do that when we can visit the restaurant and have a proper lunch with wine. With an hour- and-a-half, we, too, choose the later course. The room is packed with patrons, bus driver included. We watch to see how many times his

208

wine glass empties. Far as we can tell, it doesn't. And we prefer that version to the idea that our driver's glass might have been refilled every time we looked.

With that encouragement we board the bus at a little after one-thirty and stop again at another *autoroute* rest stop for coffee at three. Then again at a quarter past four for ten minutes only, on the side of the road. Is there a problem with the bus? No. We must wait. We realize the reason when the bus pulls beside the *rendez-vous* point, the Eltville firehouse. It arrives precisely at five o'clock. Timing is everything.

* * *

The Gallic hordes pile out of the bus and into the waiting hugs and kisses of our German hosts. Most of these people have been members of the group and shared visits back and forth for several years. The warmth comes from more than the bright July sun.

We two Americans hover by the mother ship like abandoned babies on the orphanage steps. No one claims us. We manage to get Monsieur, the Committee President's, attention, who consults his German counterpart's list and says, *pas de problème*, our German hosts have been delayed but they'll be here. So while everyone else clasps hands and exchanges *bisous* and sweeps cheerily into the firehouse for a welcome toast, we loiter beside the bus and try to look busy. We recover our bags from the belly of the bus and sift through the dozens of wine packages piled on the asphalt beside it. We find a three-pack of wine with a dented cardboard corner that looks familiar. We are ready to present it, but we are still unclaimed. We must have looked lost because our group leader re-checks the long list. Hmm. The couple named *Kelz*. Are they here? *Non.* But at least we have a name. That's a good sign that perhaps someone will be responsible for us. Hopefully, we won't sleep in the firehouse tonight.

Finally we join the remnants of people wandering up the stairs to the meeting hall. Wine and cheese and crackers are arrayed on tables. That would raise our spirits, except no one is helping themselves. The first of the welcoming speeches begin. We stand like wallflowers, eyeing the wine and crackers and hoping the speeches will be brief.

The wine is still in its bottles and the second speech has just begun when the crowd parts like the Red Sea. Those who know our situation as the unclaimed guests point. *Voila!* Our hosts have arrived. A handsome 50-something couple, each silver-haired, each over six feet tall, enter and take us in hand. They start speaking French and pause. We reply slowly. We are stumbling. The couple knows that their French is good but we look puzzled. The noisy crowd presses tightly around us.

"American" we say over the effusiveness.

The couple look at each other, then back at us. *Amerikaner?*

We are the official representatives of our French town, *oui*.

But we don't speak French well. We don't speak German at all. They solve the language problem by offering us a drink

***

The speeches wound down and the wine bottles emptied. The cheese platters were relics of cracker bits and browning munster cheese. Gradually the room acquired more space as groups gathered luggage and headed home with their hosts.

Through a combination of French, English and John's high school German we head down the street, trailing our weekend bags behind us. Our host and hostess accept the three-pack of wine, thereby solving the problem of who is to carry it. Erhard leads the way, explaining that the house is just a block away.

Voila, he says. "There's the house."

It is not a house. It is a mansion of three stories, with a massive brick façade, columns, and capacious front porch. The property surrounding it appears to cover acres as we tote our bags up the front sidewalk.

Were these people dot.com millionaires or what?

Erhard and Gudrun explain that they are resident managers for the property, which belongs to a German wine distributor. They put on the dinners for conferences and business meetings held at the property. Ah, so we wouldn't be hob-nobbing with the rich and famous, then. Erhard is a retired *chef de cuisine* who had worked for an American movie producer with a home in Monaco. Erhard isn't above name-dropping. He had met Charlie Chaplin and Gary Cooper.

Erhard may have retired from paid duty but not from continuing the tradition of creating fine cuisine. The dinner of four delicious courses, including a mouth-watering mushroom sauce on the perfectly prepared chicken, is served with proper wines.

At ten-thirty we settle back, replete. In a brief lull Gudrun gathers up dishes and Erhard serves coffee in china cups. They won't let us help. I wonder what the others in our group had for dinner and smile to myself. Somehow, we had pulled the best straw when it came to drawing potential German hosts.

"Would you like to see the wine cellar?" Erhard asks.

It's amazing, I think, how close the Germans are to the French when it comes to displaying their little wine caves. We have seen plenty of them by now and with full stomachs it is comfortable to sit here and digest, but Erhard's is a leading question.

"Of course," John and I reply on cue. I try not to yawn. The wine Erhard served had been superb. We will see the little wine cellar where it had lived before giving its life to our enjoyment.

Erhard leads the way. John and I follow with Gudrun trailing behind. She is polite but she doesn't speak French or English as well as Erhard so she appears shy. Occasionally, she tries to provide an explanation on a painting or the carving around a lintel. We don't understand much but we nod as though we do. It doesn't pay to stifle potential friendships.

We drift down the curving mahogany stairs from the third-floor apartment. We pass through massive halls with twenty-foot high ceilings. We pause along the way for a detour to the wine distributor's conference room. Erhard points out the art nouveau light fixtures and moldings on the walls. The floor is parquet. The solid mahogany table seats twenty.

We step across the front hall and enter a kitchen capable of preparing a feast for those twenty people and then some. It includes a gleaming stainless steel range the size of the Queen Mary, two large ovens, and a restaurant-size refrigerator. Erhard doesn't pause. He skirts the edge of the room and enters a hall on the other side that's the size of our living room at home. On the far side of the hall, taking up most of that wall is …

A garage door? What is a garage door doing inside the house?

Erhard pushes a button to the right of the door. It splits in two horizontally, revealing a rusty grill that grumbles open.

This mammoth service elevator will apparently take us into the depths of the house. It looks old and creaky and all four of us are to enter the elevator together, going who knows where, in a house locked up, at almost eleven at night. Shouldn't someone stay behind to call the repairmen if something goes bump in the night?

Apparently I am the only one nervous enough to consider this a problem. Erhard and Gudrun simply herd us inside. Erhard pushes a button on a panel that looks as though it came from the same era as the art nouveau conference room. Nice for furnishings but not a comforting thought for elevators.

The machine rumbles down with a view through the rust-rimmed grate to rough-hewn rock walls. Periodically the view changes and the wall seems to have disappeared but, hard as we try, all we can see is dark space. One level. Two levels. Three levels. This is no place for a claustrophobic.

The machine thumps to a stop. Erhard opens the grate and reaches his full six feet three to flip a high light switch. One dim light bulb goes on above the elevator exit. Beyond it, wrought iron wall sconces reminiscent of a Phantom of the Opera set are filled with candles and amazingly, they're already lit.

Massive stone columns support wide stone arches in a cavernous space that is punctuated with ceiling-high wooden kegs suitable for a Bacchus of mammoth thirst. The rough stone walls look like what we'd seen through the elevator grate but most of them are covered by floor to ceiling wine racks reaching up thirty or forty feet. The floor is thick stone fitted in a geometric pattern of grays.

A candle flickers cozily on top of a small, waist-high barrel, making spooky shadows on the walls and pillars. Beside the candle are four wine glasses and a bottle of white wine. With a merry smile, Erhard comments that the resident ghost has prepared an after dinner drink for their guests.

"Pooh, pooh," Gudrun says on the side. "Erhard came down in secret after dinner to prepare."

As he lifts the cork and begins to pour the wine Erhard comments that the wine is 20-year old *Eiswein* from his private stock.

John's mouth drops open. Erhard explains that *Eiswein* is made from grapes that have been left on the vine until the very last minute, just until the first freeze. Thus, the term, "Ice Wine." It's a chancy process for the vintner before he loses a lot of grapes to the cold by waiting that long. But the grapes that make it are packed with extra sugar, creating a special vintage.

(A few days later we try to buy some *Eiswein.* The price in the high three figures frightens us off more than any ghost.)

Erhard explains that the caves – and there are three levels like the one we are standing in -- held three million bottles of wine when the wine distributor ran operations here. Most of the caves, unfortunately, are now empty because the distributor is planning to sell the premises.

"But the ghost will remain," Erhard promises. The massive 18th century stone walls seem appropriate for a crypt. Hopefully any ghost is a friendly Casper who merely likes to warm up with a cozy *Eiswein* now and then.

33
OUR FIRST *Noël*

The term, *le Réveillon,* first showed up on an advertising circular left in our mailbox in late November. The word then appeared in vivid red letters on a banner that trailed above the supermarket entrance. It sprawled in gold filigree lettering in beauty shops and purple prose in the ladies' boutique.

Réveillon. It sounds like a brand of cosmetics but when it appears on hand-lettered signs in the bakery window, we know we've misinterpreted. Then our French friends begin asking what we will *do* for it.

Le Réveillon has nothing to do with lipstick and everything to do with celebrating Christmas or New Year's Eve in France. The basic idea is to party throughout the night – and the longer you can party into the wee hours the better. It's an excuse to extend eating, drinking, and conversing for an even longer period of time than the already long French lunch or Sunday dinner.

We, however, are Americans. And we're Americans of a certain age. The last time we stayed up all night Nixon was President. He didn't last either.

Nonetheless, we are in France and we intend to make the most of the experience. Naively, we jump at any opportunity to gain insights into this cultural phenomenon. This is a general attitude though whether we would work hard to implement it and lose sleep is still up in the air.

The decision was made for us.

We had just returned from a visit with our family in the States the end of October so we wouldn't return for Christmas and New Year's. Our friends Christiane and Pierre know that we are staying in the Loire countryside. It would be our first holiday in France and the first away from our family. They, themselves, are not going to venture out to visit their son in Paris this year.

Bien sûr, Christiane enthuses, we should celebrate *le Reveillon* together at their house. It is a month prior to the big event. She already appears festive in a low-cut leopard-skin blouse and skin-tight Capri pants. Her exuberance is daunting and we tentatively agree to share this Christmas dinner extravaganza before we realize that American guests will be arriving a few days before the holidays. By that time, John and I are beginning to waver in our enthusiasm. Someone else has just explained the premise of the evening, which is to greet the dawn.

The implications dawned on us.

We are about to embark on an all-night eating and drinking binge to last ten hours, the last six of which will be past our bedtime, during which time we will be required to make scintillating conversation with a couple that we don't know very well. And we will have to do it in French. The unexpected presence of our American guests, who don't speak French – not one iota -- will provide the excuse to modify the plans to something more manageable. With light heart, I telephone Christiane and tell her about the guests.

"*Pas de problème*," she says as the solution trips easily off her tongue: "Since you have visitors, the party will be at your house."

She adds that she will contribute the traditional dessert, a *bûche de Noël*. Pierre will bring the wine. That only leaves us with everything else.

I hang up the phone and tell John the good news. What a rare opportunity we've been given to throw ourselves into a traditional French holiday. We begin research into the proper French *Reveillon*. To our dismay the tradition calls for a meal that appeared more daunting in scope than Marie Antoinette could have managed with a staff of hundreds. She tried to simplify with a casual "let them eat cake" statement. Shows you the results of a cavalier attitude.

Ours is anything but cavalier. We study the menu plans. The first course, according to our advisors, Pierre and Christiane, should be *foie gras*. That means *foie gras* for six. Gulp. This platter of gold isn't going to be donated from Daniel's mom.

We don't want to cheap out on the very first course. And we are celebrating our first *Reveillon* in France, sharing it with real, not Memorex, French guests. And real American visitors. We have to do this properly. We order the *foie gras* to be picked up the day of the event. We don't ask the price.

Next on the menu. The oysters. They are also traditional, according to Christiane. I get the distinct impression she likes them and anything she likes will fit tradition. But John likes *les huitres* also so he doesn't question including them. We will serve oysters.

John and I determine turkey would be nice since we'd missed it at Thanksgiving. It will cover six nicely. We visit the most popular butcher shop in town, one known for its quality, to order a fresh turkey. The shop is bustling with activity and holiday spirits. Above the two counters the *proprietaires* have strung their holiday decorations. Hanging from their feet, like the laundry line of a serial killer, are ducks and geese and turkeys and pheasants – each decorated with lavish green and red taffeta ribbons around its neck. Their bodies have been denuded of feathers. The heads remain as intact as a dead head can be, ensuring that no one would mistakenly choose the snowy-headed duck when they want a stuffed pheasant.

We buy more French baguettes than we need and leave them to get stale for homemade dressing. We would have cranberries, of course. It's not turkey without cranberries. We don't see them in the local market stalls so we know it's time to look up the word so we can ask for them.

The word 'cranberries' does not exist in our five-pound French dictionary.

The items themselves do not exist in our usual supermarket so we visit another one across the river. Nope. Oh, well, we sigh, we'll just have to go to the big city. We take a morning especially to drive to the big city of Tours where we can shop at the giant Continent *hypermarché*. If anyone has cranberries, they will.

They don't.

We e-mail a friend in Paris. Yes, she says, cranberries are to be had in a specialty store there. Didn't I know *everything* is available in Paris? Unwritten is the comment that why aren't *I* in Paris if I want cranberries? Does she want me to buy them and mail them?

Wait, I tell her. I have another idea that will save the postage. Our Atlanta friends are coming for the holidays. Their hostess gift, I inform them, will be two packages of fresh cranberries.

***

During the innocence of the first discussions, we don't quite understand the depths of sleep deprivation we are about to undergo to celebrate *le Réveillon*. Gradually clues appear. When I suggest that we begin our celebration at seven with *apéritifs*, Christiane suggests eight. She provides the schedule, ticking off the courses in rapid order, though they will not actually occur so rapidly. We will do the *apéritifs*, then the first three courses consisting of *foie gras*, the oysters, and the turkey with its accompaniments. We will take a break from the rigors of dining, she decrees, before the salad and cheese course, the dessert and the coffee, in order to attend Christmas Eve Mass at ten o'clock at the church at the end of our street. There is just one hitch to her plan.

Our holiday guests from Atlanta are Jewish.

When they arrive, we tell them Christiane's plan and suggest that if they want to stay home we understand. We'll even stay with them, though I am looking forward hearing the Christmas hymns. They, however, want to come with us. They will see what a French Catholic Christmas is all about.

218

Thus, after champagne and enough red wine to wash down *foie gras*, oysters, turkey and all the trimmings, the six of us gather coats and totter the two blocks down the street, the ladies weaving not so much from the wine as from the high heels we've worn for this special occasion. The night is more than crisp. An arctic wind is bearing down on the Loire and we arrive at the massive church doors feeling like icicles. We hurry up the stone steps, enter the heavy oak doors and anticipate the warmth of the season in literal terms.

Instead, six icicles enter a clammy freezer. We now know why this church is called the "summer church" and the one in town the "winter church." The one in town can be heated. The only time the church on this end of town is used in winter is Christmas Eve.

It's colder inside the damp stone church than it is outside. Instead of being blown away by the wind, our breath hovers in icy repose. The cold soaks under winter coats and into flimsy holiday dresses and past the men's sport coats. It is a frigidity that wakes us from a sweet, dinner and wine soaked stupor to the cold reality of misery.

We huddle in hard wooden pews for fifteen minutes until the service begins. More precisely, the preliminaries begin. Christmas Mass proves to be comparable to Christmas dinner. Lots of courses. The choir sings a long series of songs I don't recognize. I look down the bench toward Christiane and Pierre on my left, hoping they'll look as cold as I do. Would they stay for the full hour and a half service after all this singing? Christiane doesn't look back at me. She is too busy waving at people she knows. I don't dare look at Marsha and Marty, just past John on my right. How would I explain to their synagogue that they died of exposure in a Catholic Church on Christmas?

As for John, I desperately hope that my partner will share in the desire to leave before we turn into champagne-flavored popsicles.

An hour later, the choir strikes up a rousing Gregorian chant. My arms are crossed, my knees pulled up under my wool coat that feels light as cotton. Marsha's knees are bouncing up and down under her coat as she taps her feet on the footrest. Pierre is sitting back on the hard bench, his face a mask of pain. Christiane says something to him. He responds and she turns to me. "Pierre's back is troubling him on the hard bench. He'll have to stand up and go outside."

"We can't leave him alone in pain," I say. "We can all go back to the house."

The plan is whispered to Marsha who passes it along to Marty. They look as though they'd leap tall buildings to get out, but politely refrain. Instead, the next time the worshippers stand, the six of us slide out and down the aisle, escaping into the warmth of the below-freezing night.

***

The walk home prepares us for the cheese course with red wine. It serves its medicinal purpose. The shivering stops. Then Christiane presents the *bûche de Noël*, a white roll cake around a chocolate mousse filling, topped with chocolate frosting and imitation ivy leaves on top. It is supposed to look like a log, albeit a creamy, sweet, and highly calorific one.

Coffee follows. John offers everyone a *digestif*. Everyone accepts.

Ahh, dinner is over. We've made it through with guests who do not speak French and guests who speak only a smattering of English and Christiane and Pierre used up all the words they know in the first half of the evening, prior to Mass. Still, the evening continues. We play music and talk about Pierre's favorite singer, Frank Sinatra. I bring out chocolates to give our mouths more gainful employment. No one is hungry but everyone takes one. It gives us something to fill our mouths and the lull in conversation. I make more coffee -- decaf.

It is three in the morning. Marsha lists to one side. Marty is upright but his eyes glaze over like a zombie from a grade B horror movie. Marsha's eyes close. She rouses herself enough to offer their apologies. Perhaps it is the jet lag. But please excuse them. They have to turn in.

I sigh in relief. There it is. "Have a good night," we throw after our American friends. They don't look back.

"What a lovely evening," I say. That's how sure I am that Christiane and Pierre will now make their departure. I look at my watch. So do Christiane and Pierre. They now realize the time.

And it isn't late enough.

Le Reveillon can't possibly be *terminé* at only three a.m. We sit. We chatted about something, but I'm not sure what it was. By this point, John has dropped out of the conversation entirely and I have no memory of what we may have talked about. I offer after-dinner drinks to have something to do. It might also clue them to say, '*Non, merci*, we must be leaving.'

They don't. At least the passing of the drinks provides something to talk about as we explain the various choices and discuss them in interminable detail. An hour passes. John and I look across the table at each other in desperation. My eyes are sandpaper. The kitchen is a mess of dirty plates from six courses.

Pierre hems and haws, then comments that he is sorry about his back, but it is aching again. He apologizes profusely but he will have to quit the party early. Christiane looks disappointed but agrees. It is made easier on her when John and I commiserate generously with Pierre. We are amazingly concerned. We assure him that we understand completely. It is essential he rest his back. At home. In bed.

It is four in the morning. We have *almost* made it to dawn.

34
DREAM FULFILLED

Over the years we've met a host of French people as friends and neighbors. When they learn we're not Brits, but Americans, their curiosity overwhelms the usual French discretion and one question pops out of their mouths.

"*Pourquoi?*" they ask in astonishment. "Why are you here?"

Implicit in the question are all the assumptions that the French in particular, and Europeans in general, hold about our powerful country across the ocean. They've heard about the mega shopping centers (where, of course Americans can afford to buy whatever they want, since all Americans are rich, *bien sûr*.). They've read about Hollywood movie stars. They see repeats of U.S. television depicting *Dallas* mansions. And, in a more realistic vein, they only have to read the news to envy the lower unemployment rates in the states. That alone makes the U.S. a land of opportunity to people from a country that's known unemployment recently of 10% or more. Why, oh why, would an American choose to live in France?

I begin trying to explain why we wanted an adventure and why we chose France in particular. Our comments are true, but begin to sound trite, when we extol the culture and history, the scenic beauty, the cuisine, and wine.

The younger people shake their heads in disbelief. We are either crazy or they misunderstood our bad French. Everyone knows that the U.S. has wonderful jobs where everyone makes $250,000 a year, blue jeans cost ten dollars, and New York City and Hollywood are just waiting to share their glamour and movie stars. Seen through French eyes, America is the land of milk, honey, and cowboys.

Sometimes, however, a person of *un certain âge*, meaning closer to our years, understand that we were simply seeking "*la vie,*" a way of life. How else can one wrap up everything that France offers for a person starved, not just for cheese and baguettes, but for a life that creates moments of simple pleasure rather than one of pressure and monetary pursuits.

Sure, we drove a ten-year-old *Citroën* that was silver gray like John's sideburns and slightly dented on one side, like my thighs. But it had the strength of a plow horse and got us where we were going.

We like getting up in the morning knowing that we don't have to contend with rush hour traffic. Our worst traffic jam in the French countryside develops on a narrow route through the vineyard where we slow our bikes to avoid the lumbering tractor in front of us.

When we were working in the States, we were swamped with fifty-hour work weeks, family responsibilities, and the typical striving for symbols of success. I remember many times waking in the middle of the night with dream remnants still floating in my head. "The dream recurred irregularly, but it occurred often over several years. "Your subconscious is trying to tell you something," said me to myself.

Always it concerned a simple house, unprepossessing from the street. I'd enter the front door and begin to explore. I'd open a door on the right and it would lead down a long corridor, a corridor far too long for the size house I had entered. I'd come to a short flight of stairs, mount them, and suddenly a magical space appeared. In one dream it was a conservatory filled with orchids and palm trees. In another, a passageway appeared out of nowhere, turned a corner and opened up to an attic-like room, slightly dusty with miniscule cobwebs on the overhead beams, though it wasn't dirty or frightening. The opposite. The space was reminiscent of a fine antique store. Scattered about were furniture and oil paintings, stacked against walls and leaning against a couch, with smaller treasures sitting on tabletops and hidden within mahogany chests of drawers and leather trunks.

The surprises were never of riches in the traditional sense. They were fascinating objects, in previously unknown space. The sense of wonder and exploration was that of a child seeing the the world unfold and marveling at the simplest things.

One day, several years after we arrived in France, I realized that the dream hadn't recurred -- not any permutation of it -- since we'd been here. Amateur as my analysis may be, I'm convinced that the dream ceased because the dream came true. John and I explored beyond a life that was becoming routine. We turned a corner of our lives and made fresh discoveries. We mounted old-world steps and were rewarded with new vistas and new approaches to life.

Our lives, if not our wallets, were enriched with new friends, a new language, and a new outlook on the world.

Whatever happens in the future, a part of ourselves will always belong to France. Our reincarnation gave us a French *joie de vivre*, if not the perfect French accent. Our nearsighted, over-fifty eyes saw the world from a new perspective. We learned to appreciate long leisurely conversations with friends during the lengthy dinners that went with them. We learned to discount the materialistic in favor of enjoying the moment. We gained a global viewpoint that recognizes the inter-relations between people and countries, with an understanding of the need to cooperate with each other. We opened our minds and they expanded to include the world.

We gave ourselves an incredible opportunity to discover new friends, travel, and gain insights on other ways of life. We will remember.

Made in the USA
Middletown, DE
05 September 2020

17843230R00137